Tangled Legacy

Turning Estate Planning Mistakes into Successes

TIM GORMAN

Limit of Liability/Disclaimer of Warranty:

While the author and all involved in the production of this manuscript have taken reasonable precautions in preparing this book, they assume no responsibility for any errors or omissions and make no representations or warranties with respect to the accuracy or completeness of the contents. Laws and practices vary from state to state and from country to country and change from time to time. Because each situation is different, the reader is advised to consult with his or her personal advisor regarding that individual's situation. Neither the author nor anyone involved in the production of this manuscript shall be liable for damages arising from any errors or omissions in this book.

Transactions related to estate planning and real estate require entering into legally binding contracts, with legal and taxable consequences. This book is not intended to dispense legal advice or tax advice. The reader is advised to consult with legal counsel for legal advice and with tax counsel for tax advice.

Any references to any organizations or websites does not mean that the author or anyone involved in the production of this manuscript endorses the information or organization or recommendations those entities may make.

Copyright ©2024 by Timothy Gorman, Brea, California

All right reserved.

No part of this book may be reproduced, stored in a retrieval system, or transmitted by any means, electronic, mechanical, photocopying, recording, or otherwise, without written permission from the author or the author's designated representative.

ISBN: 9798333511614

E-Mail: info@dgrealtyadvisors.com
Website: dgrealtyadvisors.com

For ordering information or special discounts for bulk purchases, please contact:

DG Realty Advisors at P. O. Box 325, Brea, CA 92822, 714.255.9998

Dust Jacket & Page Layout Design by Pavel Stanishev
Copy Editing & Production Management by Jaime M. Nies

Contents

Foreword 8
Acknowledgements 10
Preface 11
Chapter 1: Navigating the Unknown – The Legacy We Weave 16
1.1 Exploring Family Dynamics 18
1.2 Differentiating Estate Planning from Legacy Planning 20
1.3 Starting the Planning Journey 21
1.4 Role of the Executor vs. Successor Trustee 23
Chapter 2: Laying the Foundation – Crafting Your Legacy Blueprint 25
2.1 Start Planning Early and Correctly 28
2.2 Setting Financial Goals and Aspirations 31
2.3 Assembling a Team of Experts 32
2.4 Initial Strategies for Wealth Conservation and Tax Considerations 34
2.5 Aligning Family Interests with Charitable Intentions 36
2.6 Organizing Meticulously; The Criticality of Document Management 36
2.7 Estate Planning Tools to Bypass Probate 40
2.8 Annual Reviews; Adapting to Legal, Regulatory, and Familial Changes 57
2.9 Business Entity Structures 57
2.9 (a) LLCs (Limited Liability Companies) 58
2.9 (b) Corporations (S-Corps and C-Corps) 59
2.9 (c) Partnerships (General and Limited) 59
2.10 Modern Challenges (Digital Assets & Technological Advancements) 61
2.11 Letters of Instruction 62

2.12 Impact on Beneficiary Retirement Accounts 64

2.13 The Importance of Balance 65

2.14 Funding Your Trust 66

2.15 Storing & Retrieving Your Estate Planning Documents 68

2.16 Ensuring Estate Liquidity 68

2.17 Navigating Beneficiary Designations 69

2.18 Preparing Heirs: Fostering Responsibility and Independence 71

Chapter 3: Complexities of Families – Balancing Finances with Relationships 74

3.1 Addressing the Challenges of Intricate Family Dynamics 77

3.2 Estate Planning in the Face of Cultural and Communicative Diversity 78

3.3 The Consequences of Overlooking the Personal Touch 79

3.4 Navigating Potential Familial Conflicts 80

3.5 The Art of Open Dialogue and Clear Communication 81

3.6 Maintaining Family Harmony 82

3.7 Contesting the Will or Trust 84

Chapter 4: Selecting Your Successor Trustee/Executor 86

4.1 Defining the Roles and Responsibilities of Successor Trustee and Executor 89

4.1 (a) Assembling the Trust Assets 92

4.1 (b) Collecting Receivables 92

4.1 (c) Valuation of the Trust Assets 93

4.1 (d) Managing and Investing Trust Assets 93

4.1 (e) Investing Trust Assets 94

4.1 (f) Notifying the Beneficiaries 95

4.1 (g) Payment of Debts, Expenses, and Taxes 95

4.1 (h) Distributing Trust Assets to the Beneficiaries 96

4.1 (i) Final Accounting 96

4.1 (j) Duties When Death Occurs 97

4.2 Choosing the Right Person 102

4.2 (a) Questions FOR Your Executor/Successor Trustee 106

4.2 (b) Questions FROM your Executor/Successor Trustee 108

4.3 Ongoing Learning in the Realm of Estate Planning 110

4.4 Trustee Fees and Expenses 111

4.5 Liabilities, Loyalties, Prudence and Protection 112

Chapter 5: Near Death – Embracing Transition 114

5.1 The Duality of Loss: Emotional and Administrative 117

5.2 The Importance of Health Care Directives and Family Communication 118

5.2 (a) Incapacity Planning 119

5.2 (b) Disability and Long-Term Care 120

5.2 (c) Power of Attorney and Healthcare Representatives 121

5.2 (d) Final Arrangements and End-of-Life Care 122

5.3 Coping Strategies for the Emotional Burden 123

5.4 Resources for Guiding Through the Transition 124

Chapter 6: Shortly After Death – Charting Through Turmoil 127

6.1 Immediate Actions and Precautions Post-loss 129

6.2 Emotional Dimensions of Estate Administration 131

6.3 Strategies for Managing Grief and Family Dynamics 133

6.4 Self-care and Building Resilience 135

Chapter 7: Wrapping Up a Life – Executor & Successor Trustee Duties 136

7.1 Timeline and Expectations 139

7.2 Professional Roles and Their Significance 142

7.3 The Importance of Organization 144

7.4 Communication and Documentation 145

7.5 Taxes 146

7.5 (a) Federal Income Tax 148

7.5 (b) Federal Estate Tax Exemptions 148

7.5 (c) The Gift Tax 149

7.5 (d) Generation-Skipping Transfer Tax 149

7.5 (e) Valuation of the Gross Estate 149

7.5 (f) Deductions 150

7.5 (g) Paying the Federal Estate Tax 150

7.5 (h) State and Local Income Tax 150

7.5 (i) State Death Taxes 150

7.5 (j) State Inheritance Taxes 151

7.5 (k) State Estate Taxes 151

7.6 Distribution and Final Accounting 152

Chapter 8: Reflecting on a Personal Journey – Lessons and Missteps......... 154

Chapter 9: Tools and Templates for Effective Legacy Planning 165

Chapter 10: Conclusion and Reflections 176

Glossary.. 178

About The Author... 186

This book is dedicated to you, the heirs and family members, and to those courageous enough to undertake the task of planning for a future after a loved one's departure. Created to guide you in fulfilling and honoring the legacy dreams of those you cherish, it offers insights on navigating and avoiding common missteps. May this book help ensure that the legacy left behind remains clear, untangled, and faithful to the vision intended.

Foreword

Here's a hard truth here for the 21st century: there is no silver bullet for success. In today's age of instant gratification and unbridled access to the world at our fingertips, there is a misconception that anything is possible with a click or a swipe. But it's not. There is an almost naïve, childlike fixation on immediate results that fails to incorporate the life lessons, diligence and perseverance required to succeed. But those who seek information and guidance along the way have the unique opportunity to chart their own course to success, learning firsthand the lessons of those who are further down the path.

Sometimes these lessons are shared via stories and sometimes these experiences become the stories - stories we hear, stories we see and stories we live. The best stories empower us with knowledge, insight and truth, perhaps through real-life account, giving us information or an explanation of how someone accomplished or completed a particular task or feat. An affirmation of what is possible and how to achieve, mirror or replicate a similar outcome in our own lives.

Nowhere is this more powerful than in the field of personal finance, real estate investment, legacy planning and wealth management. People crave tips, pointers and secrets to bypass the pitfalls of others in the hopes of moving forward step-by step, without the step back. It is a demand that fuels an array of podcasts, webinars, YouTube videos, books and more. But in the course of amassing a personal fortune and building a portfolio, there is so much focus on how to get there that what to do once you're there is literally an afterthought at best. Until now.

In introducing Tim Gorman's insightful book on legacy planning, I'm excited to shed light on a topic too often relegated to the sidelines. Tim's perspective differs from the typical estate planning literature authored by attorneys. With a background in multifamily real estate and portfolio planning, he offers a unique perspective shaped through hands-on experience as the successor trustee of his father's complex estate. While Tim doesn't provide legal advice, he meticulously outlines options and potential pitfalls, emphasizing the importance of knowing when and how to leverage legal counsel efficiently and effectively.

What distinguishes this book from others is its raw honesty and vulnerability. Tim fearlessly confronts the intricacies of estate planning, candidly sharing his personal successes and failures in order for readers to glean invaluable insights. As a seasoned real estate professional, I've witnessed firsthand the repercussions of neglecting estate planning—unnecessary complications and disputes that compromise, jeopardize or squander away hard-earned legacies. Tim's narrative serves as a wake-up call, emphasizing proactive planning, clear communication, and a nuanced understanding of family dynamics.

As someone who grew up in and around the investment real estate business, I saw firsthand the fortunes amassed by individuals and families over generations, and how things worked out between properties, portfolios and partnerships after that first generation passed on. I applaud Tim's courage in sharing about his family's journey and his dedication to guiding others through the estate planning maze. This book will help illuminate the path for individuals and families alike, not just in securing their financial futures but in leaving lasting legacies that will transcend generations.

Whether you're a seasoned investor or just embarking on your wealth-building journey, Tim's book is essential reading. His words will inspire action, ensuring your legacy endures and your loved ones are provided for long after you're gone.

Nicholas A. Dunlap

Founder & President, Spadra Property Company

President & Co-founder, DG Realty Advisors

Acknowledgements

As I reflect on the journey of creating this book, I am compelled to express my heartfelt gratitude to those who have been beacons of guidance and wisdom.

I must extend a special acknowledgment to Roberta Coffin of Scripa Communications. Her influence as a mentor and inspiration to both my father and me has been profound. Roberta's unique ability to infuse clarity, depth, and elegance into our writing has been instrumental throughout this journey. Her pivotal role in my father's book, "Cash in on the Myths of Real Estate," and help over the years have transformed complex ideas into accessible and engaging knowledge.

My appreciation also goes to fellow experts and advisors, including Nick Lieberman, Mortgage Broker; Steven Duringer, Attorney; Yuval Domb, CPA; Sonya Loera, my longtime assistant and businesses manager; and my neighborhood early morning cold plunge and sauna group, my outlet for stress relief, friendship and support. Their insights and expertise on complex topics have immensely enriched the content of this book, enhancing its comprehensiveness and accessibility.

I extend my deepest thanks to my wife, Janette Gorman, who has been my constant source of love and inspiration. Her support has been a cornerstone in this endeavor and many others. And to my two daughters, Grace and Elise who are after all my true legacy and life's greatest source of joy.

To everyone who has contributed to this book's creation, your support and wisdom have not only made this work possible but have also profoundly enriched the experience. Thank you.

Preface

As I sit down to pen the opening chapter of this book, I can't help but reflect on the journey that led me here. It's a journey filled with twists, turns, and the kind of unexpected surprises that life has a knack for throwing our way. But it's also a journey that has deepened my understanding of estate planning, legacy, and the delicate art of transitioning wealth.

You see, I'm not just an author on estate planning; I'm someone who has lived through it—someone who has witnessed the highs, the lows, and everything in between. My name is Tim Gorman, and this book is as much a personal narrative as it is a guide to estate planning.

My story begins with a remarkable man named Bill Gorman, my father. Bill was more than just a parent; he was a mentor, a business partner, and a key figure in my life. Together, we ventured into the world of real estate, co-owning WR Gorman & Associates, a thriving brokerage. But our journey extended beyond the realm of real estate; it extended into the intricate world of estate planning.

We shared a vision—a vision of leaving a legacy that would endure long after our time on this Earth had ended. We wanted to safeguard our family's financial future, minimize the tax burden, and support the causes close to our hearts. We believed in meticulous planning and engaged a team of experts to help us navigate the labyrinth of estate planning.

However, as we soon discovered, estate planning is not a straightforward, paint-by-numbers process. It's more like a complex puzzle with pieces that don't always fit neatly together. Our journey was filled with surprises and lessons, many of which I'll share in the chapters that follow.

In the pages ahead, we'll explore the various components of estate planning, from trusts and tax strategies to asset distribution and legacy building. But we'll do so with a twist—through the lens of someone who's made mistakes, who's faced challenges, and who's learned valuable lessons along the way.

Estate planning isn't just about numbers and legal documents; it's about people, relationships, and the stories we leave behind. It's about addressing uncomfortable conversations, proactively resolving family dynamics, and ensuring that your legacy reflects your true intentions.

So, as we embark on this journey together, I invite you to join me in navigating the uncharted waters of estate planning. Let's explore the intricacies, unravel the complexities, and uncover the hidden gems that can help you create a legacy that transcends the boundaries of time.

As we delve deeper into the world of estate planning, let my experiences be your guide, my lessons be your wisdom, and my story be your inspiration. Together, let's embark on a journey that will not only shape your financial future but also leave a lasting legacy—a legacy that truly represents the essence of who you are and what you stand for.

Welcome to the adventure of a lifetime.

A Special Note about My Father

A few years back, my father Bill Gorman, decided he wanted to write a book, *"Cash in on the Myths of Real Estate"*. The book took two years to write and was a fun and challenging father son bonding experience. One that neither of us wanted to relive any time soon. Long hours and a few "healthy" debates. Having said that, here I go again. This time solo.

The purpose of Bill's book was to share knowledge so that others can benefit from Bill (and by proxy myself) have learned. As a father and son team, we also want to provide other parents and their children with a tool that they can use to help them communicate and understand the benefits of owning income properties and continuing with the wealth building that their parents started.

My dad passed away in 2023 after a life of inspiring and teaching others. Even with his passing, I am learning from him and the experiences I am gaining acting as his successor trustee. The following summarizes my father's book preface and I thought it only fitting to use it as a muse for my own book.

While earning his MBA at Northwestern University, Bill was introduced to the case study method, which he used with great success throughout his career. However, he found that this method does lead you to questioning what others believe.

After relocating to California from Chicago in the early 60's, he missed the intellectual stimulus that he had enjoyed in the classroom, so he became a credentialed economics instructor. Soon, in addition to his day job as an engineer, he began teaching night classes at a local college.

As a first-time professor, he wanted to convey the concepts and solutions in the best possible way, so he carefully followed the instructor's manual as provided with the textbook. To his surprise, many of his students struggled and did poorly on the exams.

During his second year of teaching this same course, he devoted more of his time to trying to figure out why the students kept getting the wrong answers. He, himself, soon began to question some of the answers provided. They did not make sense.

In his third year, he had an epiphany – both the answers and the questions were wrong!

Too many of the theories did not have real world applications. When applying the case study method, the solutions proposed by these theories simply did not work in practical terms.

The writing was on the wall. He would not be an economics teacher for long. Instead, he chose to focus his time and attention to wealth building through real estate. He soon found that his ability to quantify, calculate, and determine outcomes with a fair degree of certainty rewarded him both intellectually and financially. Through investing in real estate, he achieved a level of financial independence allowed him to focus on the things that he wanted to do.

In 2010, I started helping my father with computer models with more advanced "what if" decision making capabilities (computers and typing where two skills that evaded the man his entire life). I enjoyed working with my father and quickly found the same love for numbers and real estate theory. I had been brought up around real estate, having purchased my first investment property in 2003 and had long been schooled in the writings of Robert Kiyosaki, author of Rich Dad, Poor Dad. My family even spent time in my father's office playing the adapted board game "Escape the Rat Race" on his office floor. Later I become a certified public accountant, business executive and entrepreneur so my skills fit nicely with my father and real estate. Those early experiences did a lot to shape who I am today.

My dad and I worked together to find the proper ways to help build and secure his legacy for the large blended family he had made. We met with multiple attorneys, tax professionals, financial advisors until we felt they had enough knowledge to craft bill's legacy and estate plan.

It took a few years, but the plan was set in motion using a combination of new companies, trusts and other devices that will be discussed elsewhere in this book.

We prided ourselves on helping our clients build their wealth through real estate. But that was not enough. Armed with our knowledge of legacy and estate planning, we worked with many of their clients to help them achieve their goals.

I eventually left the corporate world and joined my father as a broker full time in 2013. I learned at the foot of the master and loved our adventures in business together. We would spend countless hours analyzing, debating (some would call it arguing) and serving the needs of our clients and our own real estate portfolios. It was a great honor and privilege to spend so much time with my father.

The purpose of this book is similar but different. For you see, myself and my father could only work on one side of the equation together. We could plan, interview and replan, but we could never execute the plan. For that, sadly, my dad had to pass away. The ultimate sacrifice and last bit of love and teaching from a father to a son. This book explores what we did right and more importantly, what they got wrong in our legacy planning journey together. My father was the ultimate teacher, even in death he is sharing his experiences in hopes that his family, colleagues and friends can strive.

I will stive to be as open as I can in this book, without hurting the feelings of family members. That said, it important to acknowledge the good and the bad of anything. My father was a good man, but a complex man. Many of his personality traits and decisions were shaped in a time that I did not experience. I do not judge him for our differences, only seek to acknowledge and learn. I am positive my two girls would have similar things to say about me. We are all somewhat a product of our time.

Before We Dive In: A Quick Note

Welcome to your essential guide in navigating the complex but crucial world of estate and legacy planning! This book is not just a collection of advice; it's a friendly, engaging journey through a topic often shrouded in complexity and legalese. Designed for individuals setting up their own estate plans or stepping into roles as successor trustees or executors, this guide simplifies intricate strategies using straightforward language, relatable analogies, and a touch of humor. Here's what you can expect as you turn these pages:

- **Practical and Accessible**: This guide breaks down complex estate planning strategies into understandable and applicable insights, making it ideal for personal preparation and roles like successor trustees or executors.

- **Engaging and Relatable**: The use of plain language, sports analogies inspired by a love for softball, and humor makes learning about estate planning an enjoyable experience.

- **Dynamic, Not Exhaustive**: Consider this book your play-by-play manual, focusing on crucial topics in estate planning while acknowledging the field's vastness and ever-changing nature.

- **Real-World Insights**: "COMMON MISTAKE ALERTS" throughout the book provide real-life examples of estate planning pitfalls, complete with strategies to avoid or address them.

- **Foundational Knowledge**: The book aims to spark curiosity and lay a solid groundwork in estate and legacy planning, while suggesting professional consultation for more tailored advice.

- **Intentional Repetition**: Key information is reiterated across chapters, reflecting the interconnected nature of estate planning topics, making it easy to understand and reference.

As we embark on this journey together, get ready to arm yourself with knowledge, strategy, and a bit of fun along the way!

Chapter 1
Navigating the Unknown – The Legacy We Weave

1.1 Exploring Family Dynamics

1.2 Differentiating Estate Planning from Legacy Planning

1.3 Starting the Planning Journey

1.4 Role of the Executor vs. Successor Trustee

Chapter 1, "Navigating the Unknown - The Legacy We Weave," serves as the foundational blueprint for our journey into estate and legacy planning. Much like a seasoned coach outlines a strategy before the season starts, this chapter sets the stage for the intricate process of weaving together a cohesive and meaningful legacy.

At the heart of this chapter is the exploration of family dynamics, akin to understanding the unique players in a sports team. This exploration is critical as it influences every aspect of estate and legacy planning, from decision-making to the allocation of assets. It's about recognizing that each family, like each team, has its unique characteristics and needs.

The chapter then dives into differentiating estate planning from legacy planning. While estate planning can be likened to the tactical side of a sports game, focusing on the distribution of assets and legalities, legacy planning is about the ethos and heart of the team. It captures the values, stories, and memories that define a person's life journey.

Furthermore, the chapter emphasizes the importance of starting the planning journey early. Early planning in estate and legacy matters ensures a well-thought-out strategy that can adapt over time. It's about setting clear goals and being ready for the challenges and opportunities that lie ahead.

An essential part of this journey is understanding the roles of the Executor and the Successor Trustee. Each role is distinct yet complementary. Understanding these roles is crucial for the smooth execution of the estate plan and ensuring that the legacy is carried out as intended.

Throughout the chapter, there's a focus on integrating these various elements into a harmonious and effective plan. Emphasis is placed on blending the practical and the emotional, the legal and the personal, all coming together to create a legacy that truly reflects the essence of an individual's life and values. This foundational chapter sets the tone for the detailed exploration of these themes in the subsequent chapters, each adding depth and detail to the estate and legacy planning journey.

1.1 Exploring Family Dynamics

Welcome to a journey deeply inspired by my father, Bill Gorman, whose life story is not just a personal memoir but a rich tapestry that mirrors the complexities many families face. Bill's life, and journey with estate and legacy planning alongside myself as his on and business partner, offers a unique lens through which we can explore the intricacies of estate and legacy planning.

Bill's life began in 1935 in Chicago, where his humble beginnings did not slow his aspirations. Excelling in both sports and academics, he pursued his passions at Purdue and Northwestern, cultivating a lifelong love for softball. His favorite memories, like the one where a "300 foot" home run dented the first family car, the one he purchased for the family, capture the essence of his spirited character.

His professional journey in real estate, starting in engineering and culminating in founding his own brokerage in 1972, reflects a life of dedication growth and overcoming challenge. Even as he navigated the challenges of dementia in his later years, Bill's life story continued to be one of resilience and change, including a late life marriage that brought new layers of complexity to our family dynamics.

Like many families, ours could be accurately described as "blended". Bill's three marriages, and an inclusive approach to family, created a diverse and dynamic household. This diversity wasn't just marital; it was cultural and social.

The diversity of our family, though enriching, also introduced its share of challenges. Our family's story is a vivid example of how modern families often find themselves navigating a maze of relationships and societal changes. It's a reflection of many families' realities, where the merging of different cultures, traditions, and personal histories creates a unique blend of challenges and opportunities.

In this book, I draw parallels to similar situations in other families, recognizing that each family has its own unique story and set of complexities. The lessons learned from my father's life, especially in his later years, are shared with honesty and sensitivity. In Chapter 8, "Learning from Mistakes," I delve into these experiences.

Through this book, I aim to guide readers in navigating their estate and legacy planning, informed by the richness of diverse family dynamics and the wisdom gained from personal experiences. Let's start on this journey together, drawing inspiration and insight from the life of my father and the universal complexities of modern families.

1.2 Differentiating Estate Planning from Legacy Planning

In the game of wealth transfer, legacy and estate planning are like two players with different roles. Estate planning is the defender, guarding your assets through legal means like wills and trusts. It involves making sure your hard-earned assets reach the right hands without unnecessary loss to taxes or legal complexities.

COMMON MISTAKE ALERT: Treating estate planning as the whole game

Legacy planning is the star striker, bringing color and life to your plan. It's about the stories, values, and lessons you pass down. It involves ensuring that your legacy is more than wealth; it's also wisdom, responsibility, and heritage. Legacy planning is about founding a future, not just leaving a fund.

In this playbook, we don't just focus on numbers and legalities. We delve into your family's unique story, crafting a plan that resonates with your values and vision. So, let's create a legacy that lives on, defining the difference between merely leaving an estate and creating a lasting legacy.

Legacy Planning	Estate Planning
Focuses on leaving a lasting impact or legacy beyond finances	Focus transferring financial assets
Considers non-financial assets, family values, personal beliefs and life lessons	Financial assets such as real estate, cash and equivalents, personal property are primary consecrations
Involves estate planning elements expanded to included philanthropy, community involvement and other special arrangements and conditions	Often focuses on tax planning, asset protection and legal documentation

1.3 Starting the Planning Journey

Embarking on the journey of estate and legacy planning is much like setting sail on a voyage across the vast seas of your life's work and values. It's a voyage that navigates through your personal history, charting a course that encompasses not only your material wealth but also the narrative threads that define you. This quest is not just about financial foresight—it's about introspection, understanding that your enduring legacy is an intricate mosaic of your experiences and beliefs.

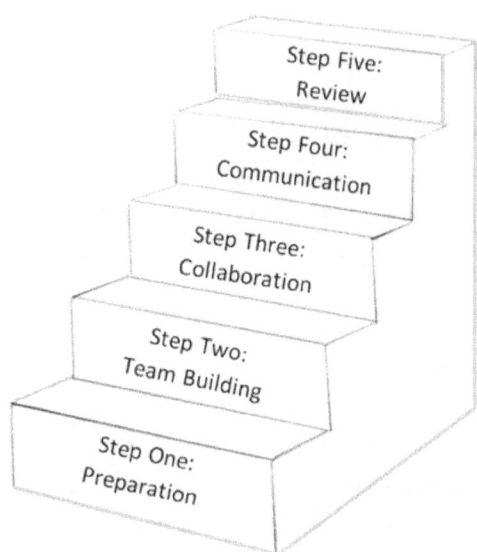

The compass for this expedition is not merely legal documents, but rather the collective wisdom gleaned from your life's journey. It's a profound look inward, acknowledging that your legacy is a rich tapestry woven from much more than the assets you will bequeath.

This book presents a Legacy Planning Guide that differentiates between tangible estate planning and the more nuanced legacy planning, highlighting the importance of aligning your life's values with your estate strategy.

COMMON MISTAKE ALERT: Failing to plan

The most perilous pitfall on this path is the failure to embark on it at all. Delaying or overlooking the creation of your estate plan can lead to your life's work being left in the hands of a probate court, a scenario fraught with uncertainty and potential strife for your loved ones.

The solution lies in seizing the day to start—or update—your estate plan. It's not about waiting for a sign or a perfect moment; it's about taking action now. Reflect on what you cherish, what you stand for, and how you envision the legacy you wish to leave behind.

The risks of postponement are too grave to be ignored. Indeed, the absence of a clear, documented estate plan can ensnare your assets in a legal limbo that may not reflect your intentions, leaving your loved ones mired in a procedural quagmire. Detailed instructions and orderly documentation can transform your estate from a potential puzzle into a clear testament of your life's intentions.

COMMON MISTAKE ALERT: Failing to avoid probate

Probate—often viewed as a game of legal hurdles—is the court-supervised process of authenticating your will and settling your estate. It's a path we strive to avoid, for it can become a public and protracted legal affair, with the potential to erode your estate's value through fees and to diminish your privacy.

Failing to craft a comprehensive estate plan is akin to walking a tightrope without a safety net, where one misstep can plunge your estate into the complexities of probate. It's a scenario where the courts, not your carefully considered choices, may determine the fate of your assets, possibly leading to outcomes that diverge significantly from your wishes.

To circumvent the twists and turns of probate, ensure your planning is thorough, with all i's dotted and t's crossed. Make sure your estate plan is robust, up-to-date, and clearly articulated. By doing so, you anchor your estate in the safe harbor of your making, sheltered from the storms of legal uncertainty.

In the subsequent chapters, particularly Chapter 9, we arm you with a suite of tools to steer you through the estate planning process, offering a beacon to guide you in enshrining your legacy in both spirit and letter, ensuring it's cherished and revered long after you've set sail on your final voyage.

1.4 Role of the Executor vs. Successor Trustee

In the intricate game of estate planning, it's quite common for one key individual to play dual roles: the Successor Trustee and the Executor. Imagine this dual role like a multi-talented athlete who's both a seasoned coach and a star quarterback.

The Successor Trustee jumps into action to manage the trust when the original Trustee can't, due to illness or passing. At the same time, the Executor is charged with implementing the will, sorting out the deceased's assets and debts, and making sure the last wishes are carried out.

Sometimes, these two crucial roles are combined in one person, blending the duties of Successor Trustee and Executor. This can streamline the process significantly, ensuring a smooth and efficient execution of your estate plan.

In this book, the roles of Successor Trustee and Executor are sometimes discussed interchangeably, reflecting their overlapping responsibilities in many estate plans. While distinct in their legal definitions and specific duties, both roles share the crucial function of ensuring your wishes are honored after you're gone. As we delve into these roles, particularly in Chapter Four, keep in mind that the principles, strategies, and insights we explore apply broadly to both. This approach allows us to focus on the core lessons and strategies essential for successful estate and legacy planning, regardless of the specific title held by your chosen representative.

DIFFERENCES	Executor	Initial Trustee	Successor Trustee
Start of Work	Upon the death of the testator	Specific to end-of-life care	Upon the death or incapacity of the grantor or initial trustee
Scope of Work	The Will	The life of the Trust	
Duties	Gathers and distributes assets, settles debts, pays taxes	Ongoing trust asset management, implements terms of the trust, makes investment decisions, distributes trust assets	

Chapter 2

Laying the Foundation – Crafting Your Legacy Blueprint

2.1 Start Planning Early and Correctly

2.2 Setting Financial Goals and Aspirations

2.3 Assembling a Team of Experts

2.4 Initial Strategies for Wealth Conservation and Tax Considerations

2.5 Aligning Family Interests with Charitable Intentions

2.6 Organizing Meticulously; The Criticality of Document Management

2.7 Estate Planning Tools to Bypass Probate

2.8 Annual Reviews; Adapting to Legal, Regulatory, and Familial Changes

2.9 Business Entity Structures

    (a) LLCs (Limited Liability Companies)

    (b) Corporations (S-Corps and C-Corps)

    (c) Partnerships (General and Limited)

2.10 Modern Challenges (Digital Assets and Technological Advancements)

2.11 Letters of Instruction

2.12 Impact on Beneficiary Retirement Accounts

2.13 The Importance of Balance

2.14 Funding Your Trust

2.15 Storing & Retrieving your Estate Planning Documents

2.16 Ensuring Estate Liquidity

2.17 Navigating Beneficiary Designations

2.18 Preparing Heirs: Fostering Responsibility and Independence

Chapter 2 of our journey into estate and legacy planning is all about laying a strong foundation for the future. Think of it as the preseason training for your estate planning team, where preparation, strategy, and foresight are key.

In this chapter, we emphasize the importance of starting early. Just like in sports, the earlier you start training, the better prepared you are for the game. Early planning in estate matters gives you the advantage of time to make thoughtful decisions, explore various strategies, and adjust your plans as life evolves.

We delve into the art of setting financial goals and aspirations, akin to a coach setting the season's objectives. It's important to understand what you want to achieve with your wealth, both for yourself and for future generations.

An essential part of this process is assembling your dream team of experts. This includes legal, financial, and tax professionals who bring their specialized skills to the table, ensuring that every angle of your estate plan is meticulously crafted and executed.

We also tackle the crucial aspects of wealth conservation and tax planning. Just as a sports team strategizes to defend and optimize its strengths, we explore ways to protect your assets and minimize tax liabilities.

Aligning family interests, particularly when intertwined with charitable inclinations, is another focus area. It's about ensuring that your legacy reflects your values and contributes positively to the community and causes you care about.

Organizational skills are key. Like maintaining a well-organized playbook, keeping your documents in order and conducting regular reviews of your estate plan ensures that you stay on top of legal, regulatory, and familial changes.

In this digital age, we also address modern challenges like digital assets and technological advancements, ensuring that your estate plan is robust and relevant in today's world.

Lastly, we highlight the importance of Letters of Instruction. These are personal notes that guide your successors, much like a coach's advice to players, ensuring that your wishes are understood and respected. Throughout this chapter, we aim to equip you with the knowledge and tools necessary to build a strong, flexible estate plan that stands the test of time and change, much like a well-trained, adaptable sports team ready for the season ahead.

2.1 Start Planning Early and Correctly

Embarking on your legacy planning journey early is like pre-season training in sports – it's essential to be prepared before the season begins. You need to get to know your players, test your strategies and be ready to make changes over a long season. This process isn't just a legal formality; it dives deep into your family's unique history, values, and dynamics, setting you apart from others. Early planning allows you to develop a flexible, evolving strategy, avoiding the pitfalls of hurried, last-minute decisions.

COMMON MISTAKE ALERT: Starting with an attorney

While lawyers are crucial, beginning your journey solely with legal counsel might not fully capture your family's unique story. It's like a coach crafting a game plan without knowing the players. First, outline your legacy goals with your family, then find an attorney who aligns with your vision and can translate it into an effective estate plan.

Attorneys, skilled in law, might not fully grasp the unique tapestry of your family's values, goals, and dynamics. They may offer standard plans that don't resonate with your unique vision. Attorneys vary in expertise, approach to risk, client interaction, and overall philosophy. Their office size and the attention they can provide also differ. Thus, define your legacy goals first within your family, then seek an attorney who can transform these into a tangible, effective estate plan, ensuring your legacy plan is a true reflection of your life and values, not just a legal document.

The best place to start is within. Ask yourself the following and keep a written record of your goals and desired legacy.

Question 1: What is your desired legacy?

- Financial security for future generations.
- Charitable contributions and philanthropic impact.
- Preservation of family traditions and values.
- Creation of a family foundation or trust.
- Establishing educational scholarships.

Question 2: What specific goals do you wish to achieve?

- Minimizing estate taxes.
- Avoiding probate and ensuring a smooth transfer of assets.
- Providing for the financial needs of your spouse and children.

- o   Protecting assets from creditors or lawsuits.
- o   Preserving family wealth and minimizing the risk of squandering.

Question 3: How do you envision the distribution of your assets among your beneficiaries?

- o   Equal distribution among all beneficiaries.
- o   Providing for specific needs or circumstances of each beneficiary.
- o   Designating a primary beneficiary with contingency plans alternates.
- o   Creating a trust to manage and distribute assets over time.
- o   Considering the age and financial responsibility of beneficiaries.

Question 4: Have you considered any charitable giving or philanthropic endeavors?

- o   Donating a percentage of your estate to specific charities or causes.
- o   Establishing a charitable foundation or trust to support ongoing philanthropy.
- o   Naming charities as beneficiaries of certain assets.
- o   Setting up a fund for family involvement in charitable giving decisions.
- o   Exploring impact investing to align your estate with your philanthropic goals.

Question 5: Are there any specific family considerations or concerns?

- o   Providing for the financial needs of minor children or dependents.
- o   Addressing potential conflicts among family members or beneficiaries.
- o   Ensuring care and financial support of special needs family members.
- o   Balancing the interests of a blended family or multiple marriages.
- o   Appointing guardians for minor children or dependents.

Question 6: Have you thought about potential tax implications and how to minimize them?

- o   Establishing a revocable living trust to avoid probate and potential estate taxes.
- o   Making use of lifetime gift tax exemptions to transfer assets.
- o   Utilizing tax-efficient strategies.
- o   Considering the impact of state and federal estate taxes on your assets.
- o   Seeking professional advice from an estate planning attorney or tax specialist.

Question 7: How can your heirs best honor your vision and goals as the executor?

- Implement your estate plan faithfully.
- Communicate effectively with beneficiaries.
- Seek professional guidance when needed.
- Preserve and protect estate assets.
- Maintain impartiality and fairness in asset distribution.

Question 8: How do you wish to handle your digital legacy?

- Cataloging and arranging for the transfer or closure of digital accounts.
- Providing access to digital assets like social media, emails, and online banking.
- Ensuring continuity or termination of online businesses and digital content.

Question 9: What are your healthcare preferences in case of incapacity?

- Designating a healthcare proxy to make decisions on your behalf.
- Establishing clear instructions for long-term and end-of-life care.
- Creating advanced healthcare directives and living wills.

Question 10: How do you want to be remembered and celebrated?

- Outlining preferences for funeral, memorials, or celebrations of life.
- Establishing funds or plans for commemorative events or legacy projects.
- Recording personal history, stories, and messages for future generations.

Question 11: What plans do you have for your business succession?

- Identifying and grooming a successor or setting up a sale or closure plan.
- Planning for the continuation or dissolution of business interests.
- Structuring buy-sell agreements and funding methods for business transition.

Question 12: How will you ensure your pets are cared for after you're gone?

- Establishing a pet trust or making formal arrangements.
- Allocating funds for the pet's care and outlining care instructions.
- Selecting alternate caregivers.

Question 13: What steps have you taken to secure your estate against legal disputes?

- Engaging in thorough documentation and clear communication of your wishes.
- Creating mechanisms within your plan to resolve potential disputes.
- Ensuring all estate planning documents are legally sound and up-to-date.

COMMON MISTAKE ALERT: Starting too late

Delaying legacy planning until incapacity or after a family member has passed is like missing the entire pre-season. You lose the chance for direct conversations and clear understanding, often leading to rushed decisions and oversights.

Starting early ensures you are prepared. Yet, early starts don't guarantee perfection. Miscommunications and avoiding tough talks can still occur, much like a team navigating unforeseen challenges. The following sections will explore these issues, offering strategies to navigate them effectively.

2.2 Setting Financial Goals and Aspirations

Setting financial goals in your legacy plan is similar to strategizing in a baseball game. Each play, or decision, needs to be aligned with the overall game plan, considering both immediate actions and the end goal. It involves understanding the different roles each player, or family member, has and how their individual aspirations fit into the overall strategy.

COMMON MISTAKE ALERT: Zeroing in solely on accumulating assets

Just like in baseball, where focusing only on home runs can miss strategic plays, in estate planning, overemphasis on asset accumulation can overshadow other important aspects. Real estate, in our experience, has been a key player, each property offering unique potential. But it's crucial to remember that this is part of a larger game plan, balancing wealth creation with family harmony and individual goals.

2.3 Assembling a Team of Experts

Assembling your legacy planning team is indeed akin to selecting players for a championship team, where understanding each member's role and ensuring their compatibility is crucial. Knowing your resources, understanding their functions, and recognizing how the wrong choice could impact your game plan is key. Whether you need multiple tax professionals for different tax aspects or a specific kind of attorney, each choice can significantly influence the outcome. Here's a guide to each professional's role and how the wrong fit could inadvertently jeopardize your legacy planning strategy:

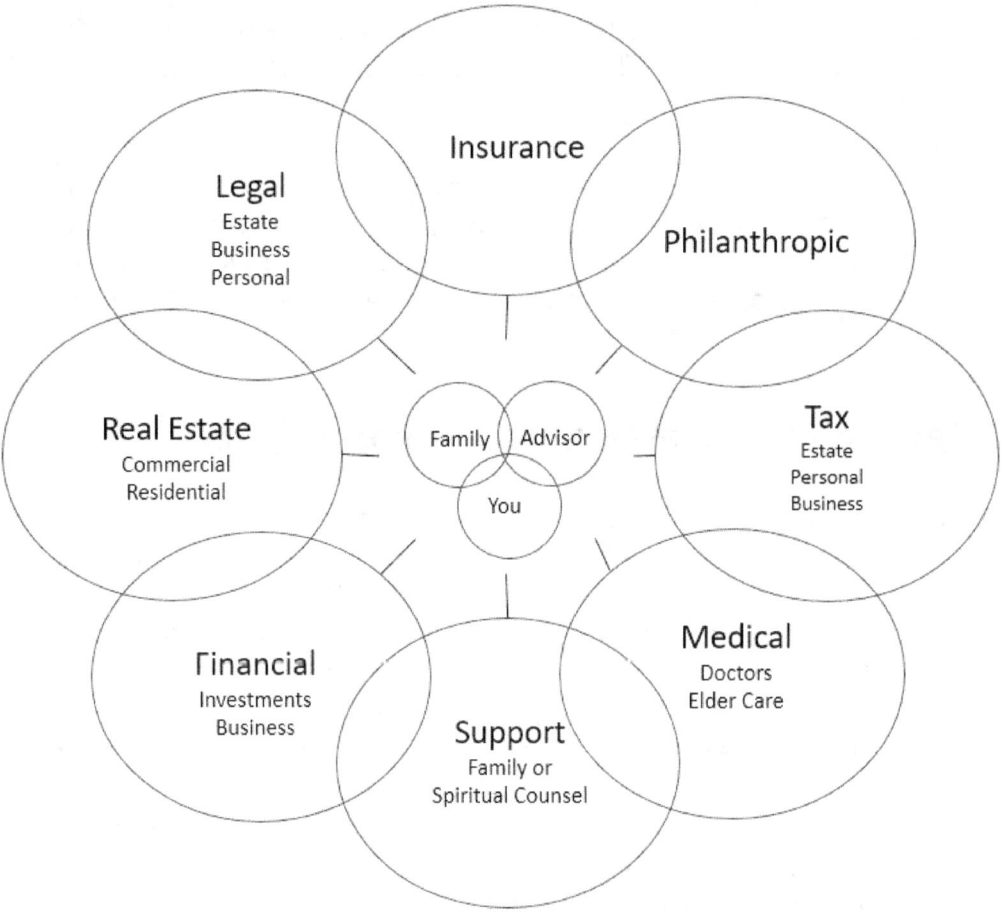

- **Attorney**: An attorney specialized in estate law provides advice on the legal aspects of estate planning and drafts legal documents like wills and trusts. The wrong attorney, unfamiliar with your specific needs and dynamics, could create a generic plan that fails to address unique family circumstances, leading to potential disputes or oversights.

- **Financial Advisor**: Manages your investments and financial strategies to align with your legacy goals. An advisor lacking in estate planning experience might miss opportunities to optimize your assets for generational wealth transfer.

- **Tax Professional:** Navigates complex estate, personal, and business taxes. Inexperienced professionals could overlook crucial tax-saving strategies, leading to higher tax burdens for your estate or beneficiaries.

- **Real Estate Expert:** Specializes in managing and strategizing real estate investments. This expert offers crucial advice on property management, investment strategies, and market trends. Their insights are vital for estates with significant real estate assets. However, selecting a professional who lacks the necessary expertise or experience in real estate can lead to missed opportunities or mismanagement. For instance, an unfamiliarity with complex property transactions such as 1031 exchanges could result in significant tax liabilities or lost growth potential, hindering your estate's financial health.

- **Family Counselor**: Assists with the emotional and psychological aspects of estate transitions. A counselor not skilled in navigating family dynamics during estate planning could fail to mediate conflicts effectively.

- **Insurance Professional:** Reviews and advises on insurance policies related to the estate. Inadequate understanding of estate planning can lead to insufficient coverage or missed opportunities in using life insurance as a strategic estate tool.

- **Business Advisor:** Focuses on business interests within your estate, including succession planning. Without expertise in transitioning business ownership, they may give advice that disrupts business continuity or ignites family disputes.

- **Philanthropic Advisor**: Helps align charitable giving with estate planning objectives. A misaligned advisor might guide you towards unsuitable charitable contributions, not reflecting your family's values.

- **Elder Care Specialist:** Offers advice on long-term care and its impact on estate planning. Lack of understanding in balancing elder care costs with estate preservation could lead to the depletion of estate assets.

COMMON MISTAKE ALERT: Choosing advisors based on personal relationships or referrals alone

Selecting friends, colleagues, or family members without proper vetting can lead to a plan that doesn't align with your goals or lacks professional rigor. Conduct thorough due diligence to ensure each advisor's expertise and philosophy align with your legacy objectives. If your buddy John had a great plan, it does not necessarily mean it will be great for you!

COMMON MISTAKE ALERT: Not questioning the source of information or advice

Just because you can do something doesn't mean you should. Attorneys, while experts in the law, may not always weigh the emotional or relational impacts of their advice. It's crucial to consider how legal decisions might affect family dynamics or lead to challenges. And remember, attorneys get paid, even in disputes. This isn't to demean their work, but it's wise to always consider the source.

The same applies to accountants. Some may favor riskier strategies, others lean conservative. Ultimately, you're the one signing off. The numbers are your responsibility, so ensure they align with your comfort level and goals.

The fit of the advisor with your personal style is as crucial as the expertise each advisor brings. Consider whether they're formal or direct, how they communicate, and if their approach aligns with your preferences. Are they from a large firm offering a wide range of services, or a smaller practice that might provide more personalized attention? How they make you feel is vital – you want advisors who not only offer sound advice but also make you comfortable and confident in your decisions. This personal fit ensures a smoother, more cohesive planning process and a legacy plan that truly reflects your family's unique story and values.

2.4 Initial Strategies for Wealth Conservation and Tax Considerations

Wealth conservation in legacy planning is like a well-coached team – it's all about strategic plays and defense. In our family's playbook, this involved setting up trusts, LLCs and employing tax-efficient strategies to safeguard and grow our assets. But wealth conservation is not just about minimizing or delaying taxes. We learned the hard way that focusing solely on tax avoidance can ruffle family feathers and skew long-term objectives.

COMMON MISTAKE ALERT: Overemphasis on tax avoidance

A successful wealth conservation strategy is more holistic. It's about striking a balance, ensuring financial gains don't come at the cost of family harmony or future goals. It's about smart plays that bolster not just your bank account but also your family's unity and legacy.

The following is a list of some popular strategies. Remember, the strategies listed here are not exhaustive and should not be viewed as a one-size-fits-all solution. Tax laws are subject to change, and the effectiveness of each strategy depends on individual circumstances. It's crucial to consult with your professional team of advisors to determine the best approach tailored to your specific needs and goals. This book offers general guidance and should be used as a starting point in your wealth conservation journey.

- **Avoiding Probate**: Think of probate like a lengthy, mandatory timeout where the court referees how your estate is handled. Avoiding probate means keeping the play in your control, away from court interference.

- **Estate Tax Avoidance**: This is akin to a defensive strategy to protect your estate from hefty tax tackles, ensuring your heirs get more of the wealth you pass down.

- **Maintaining Low Property Tax Bases**: Like negotiating for the best salary cap for your team, this involves strategies to keep property tax rates low, boosting your estate's financial health.

- **Step-Up in Basis:** It's like resetting the scoreboard at the time of your death, valuing assets at their current market rate, which can reduce the tax burden for your heirs.

- **Gifting Strategies**: Think of this as an early pass of the ball (assets) to your team members (heirs), reducing the size of the field (estate) that's subject to taxes.

- **Charitable Donations:** Like sponsoring a sports event, this tactic not only supports causes close to your heart but also offers potential tax advantages.

- **Trusts for Tax Planning:** Utilizing trusts is like having a versatile playbook for managing and passing on your assets, with plays designed to minimize tax hits.

- **Life Insurance Policies:** Life insurance can be like a star player who delivers tax-free wins (benefits) to your team (beneficiaries) when you're not there.

- **Setting Up LLCs and Other Entities:** This is like forming a subsidiary team under your main squad, managing assets in a structure that can offer tax benefits and guard against liabilities.

2.5 Aligning Family Interests with Charitable Intentions

Philanthropy in legacy planning can unite a family around a shared vision and commitment to community outreach. It's a chance to instill values of generosity and social responsibility in heirs. However, it's not a universal fit for every family.

COMMON MISTAKE ALERT: Forcing philanthropy

While there are benefits to giving, such as fostering a shared family vision and enhancing community welfare, it's essential not to impose this on a family, especially in complex, blended families with diverse needs and views. Remember, "charity begins at home" and family needs and goals come first. Any philanthropic endeavor should be a collective, fitting decision, not an obligation.

2.6 Organizing Meticulously; The Criticality of Document Management

Organizing your estate documents is crucial, much like how a coach ensures their team's playbook is always current and accessible. In our family, utilizing tools such as "Profile" and "Key Documents" from DG Realty Advisors proved vital for maintaining order. It's common to feel overwhelmed by the sheer volume of information that needs to be collected, documented, and updated regularly (refer to figures 2.6 a and 2.6 b for a detailed list by category). Fortunately, numerous tools and resources are available to facilitate organization. Your professional team can be a great starting point, offering free or cost-effective organizational methods. Additionally, I've included a brief overview of the tools I've developed in figures in Chapter 9. The key is not to be daunted by the task; start with small steps, and you'll make significant progress before you know it.

COMMON MISTAKE ALERT: Failing to keep documents current

Remember, completing your estate documents is not a one-off task. As life evolves, your documents should too. Regular updates are essential to ensure your plan remains relevant and effective. Avoid falling into complacency; treat your estate documents as living, evolving entities. They should be revisited annually or after significant life events. For more detailed guidance on maintaining organization and staying up-to-date, refer to Section 2.8.

COMMON MISTAKE ALERT: Neglecting document management and storage

The importance of this step cannot be overstated. Just as miscommunication can disrupt a game on the field, disorganized documents can derail your estate plan. Consider using a secure online storage facility for all your important documents and passwords. A variety of tools are available to help you manage and secure your information effectively. Make sure to utilize these resources. For a comprehensive list of tools and resources to assist in staying organized, delve into Chapter 9, or consult your professional advisors for customized solutions.

St Cash & Eq.	Liabilities	Retirement	Securities	Personal Items
Cash	Auto loans	401(k) plans	Annuities	Artwork
Certificate of Deposit (CDs)	Basic Living Expense	Education Savings	Certif of Deposit (CDs)	Auto
Checking / Savings Accounts	Business Loans	Defined Benefit Plans	Commodities Securities	Collections
Commodities (Gold, Silver, etc.)	Child Support	Individual Retirement Accounts	Exchange-Traded Funds (ETFs)	Furniture
Money market	Credit Card Debt	Pension	Foreign Currencies	Jewelry
Private Safe	Home equity loans/LOC	Retirement annuities	Mutual Funds	Other Personal Items
Rewards Program	Legal Judgments/ liens	Social Security	Options	
Safe Deposit Box	Mortgage	Other Retirement	Stocks & Bonds	
Treasury Bills (T-bills)	Personal Debts		Treasury Securities	
Other Cash Equivalents	Student loans		Unit Invest Trusts (UITs)	
	Tax liabilities		Other Securities	
	Rent			
	Other Liabilities			

Figure 2.6 a*: Lists key items to track a person's financial footprint. These items are all compiled in the Account List tool outlined in Chapter 9.*

Other Assets & Insurance	Bus. Int & W2 Income	Property	Investment Property	Other Investment Funds
Crypto & Digital Assets	Corporation	Family Home	Comm. Prop (Office, Retail, Warehouses)	Delaware Statutory Trusts (DSTs)
Deferred Comp	Franchise Ownership	Timeshare	Residential Property (SFR, Condos, Apart)	Real Estate Investment Trusts (REITs)
Foreign Assets	Joint Venture	Vacation Property	Medical or Healthcare Facilities	Real Estate Limited Partnerships (RELPs)
Goodwill	Nonprofit	Other Personal Property	Self-Storage Facilities	Real Estate Syndications
Inheritance *(Received or Expected)*	Partnership		Senior or Assisted Living	Other RE Investments
Insurance - Auto	Sole Proprietorship		Student Housing	
Insurance - Disability	Trust Fund		Vacant Land	
Insurance - Property	W2 Employment		Vacation or Short-term Rental	
Insurance - Life	Other Income		Other Inv. Property	
Insurance - Medical				
Intellectual Prop. *(TM, Patents, Copyrights)*				
Money Owed to You				
Royalties				

Figure 2.6 a (continued): Lists key items to track a person's financial footprint. These items are all compiled in the Account List tool outlined in Chapter 9.

Key Contracts	Personal Documents	Alarms	Locked Places
Accountant - Estate Planning	Birth Certificate	Boat	Access Card/Code
Accountant - Tax Prep & Business	Business (Articles & Bylaws, etc.)	Business	Combination Lock
Attorney - Estate Planning	Certification of Trust	House	Computer Password
Attorney - General	Deed	Vehicle	Hiding Place
Attorney - Real Estate	Drivers License	Other Alarm	Mini/Public Storage
Broker - Financial	Educational		Post Office Box
Broker - Mortgage	Employment Agreement		Safe - Private
Broker - Real Estate	Funding Instructions		Safe-Deposit Box
City	Insurance		Things Needing Keys
Cleaning Person	Marriage/Divorce		Other Password
Contractor	Military Document		
Executor - First Successor	Nuptial Agreement		
Executor - Second Successor	Passport		
Gardener	Powers of Attorney for Healthcare		
Guardians of Minors	Pre or Post Marital Agreement		
Insurance Agent	Prepaid Funeral Contract		
Medical - Dentist	Property Management		
Medical - Other	Professional		
Medical -Family Practitioner	Promissory Notes		
Pool Maintenance	Religious Ceremonial		
Property Manager	Schedules of Assets Directive to Trustees - Instruction Letter		
Religion/Faith	Settlement of Estate		
Trustee	Tax		
Vehicle Repair	Trust		
	Will		

Figure 2.6 b: *Lists key items to track a person's documents, contacts, alarms, and locked places. These items are all compiled in the tools outlined in Chapter 9.*

2.7 Estate Planning Tools to Bypass Probate

In estate planning, selecting the right tools is crucial for ensuring your wishes are respected and your estate is managed efficiently. This section provides a comprehensive overview of Trusts, Wills, and Other Common Tools used in estate planning, focusing on strategies to bypass the often-burdensome probate process.

	Estate Tax Planning	Income Tax Planning	Names Someone To Handle Your Affairs When you Pass	Names Who You Want To Receive Assets	Names Someone to Handle Your Affairs if You're Unable	Asset Protection for Heirs	Avoids Probate	Private Process
Do Nothing No Will or Trust	No	No	GOV Decides	GOV Decides	GOV Decides	No	No	No
Will Only	Yes	Limited and often not included	Yes	Yes	No	Possible, but often not included	No	No
Will & Trust	Yes	Yes	Yes	Yes	Yes	Yes	Yes	Yes

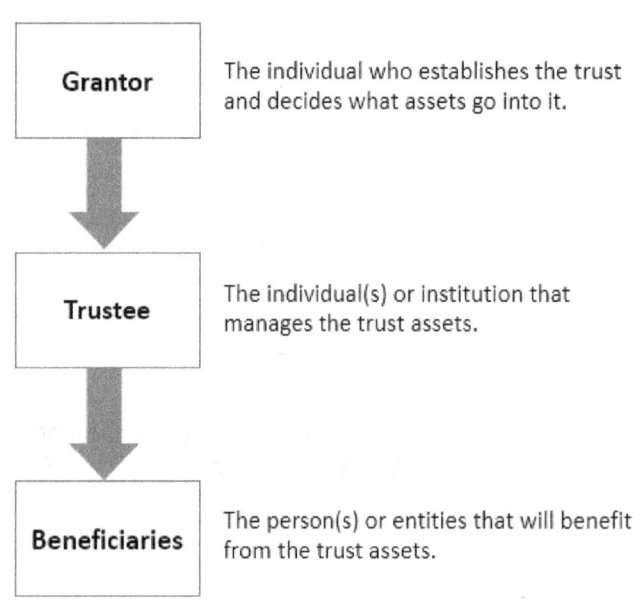

Grantor — The individual who establishes the trust and decides what assets go into it.

Trustee — The individual(s) or institution that manages the trust assets.

Beneficiaries — The person(s) or entities that will benefit from the trust assets.

Trusts

Trusts are versatile instruments in estate planning, each designed for specific purposes and circumstances. Here's a detailed look at various types of trusts:

- **Bypass Trust**: Designed to minimize estate taxes by allowing assets to bypass the surviving spouse and go directly to other beneficiaries while still providing for the spouse. Advantages include reduced estate taxes and ensuring financial support for the surviving spouse and future beneficiaries. Disadvantages are its irrevocable nature, which limits flexibility, and the complexity in setting up and administering the trust.

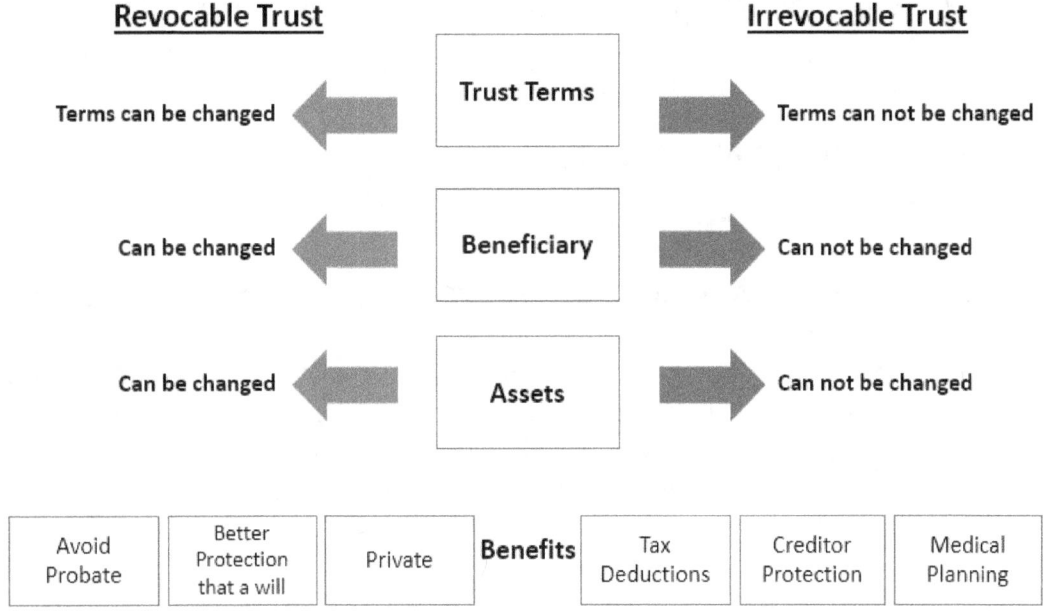

- **Revocable Living Trust**: Allows for flexible asset management and control during the grantor's lifetime, with assets transferring to beneficiaries upon death without going through probate. Advantages include the grantor retaining control and the ability to avoid probate, ensuring privacy and potentially saving on costs and delays. Disadvantages include a lack of tax benefits during the grantor's lifetime and the requirement for active management and funding.

- **Irrevocable Living Trust**: Once established, this trust cannot be altered; it is used for asset protection, estate tax reduction, and charitable giving. Advantages include providing asset protection and reducing estate tax liability, and being ideal for long-term charitable giving. Disadvantages involve the loss of control over assets placed in the trust and the complexity in establishment and management.

- **Generation Skipping Trust**: Facilitates asset transfer to grandchildren, skipping a generation to reduce estate and generation-skipping transfer taxes. Advantages include avoiding double taxation on assets passing to the next generation and protecting assets for future generations. Disadvantages are its subjection to specific tax rules and the potential for creating family conflicts or misunderstandings.

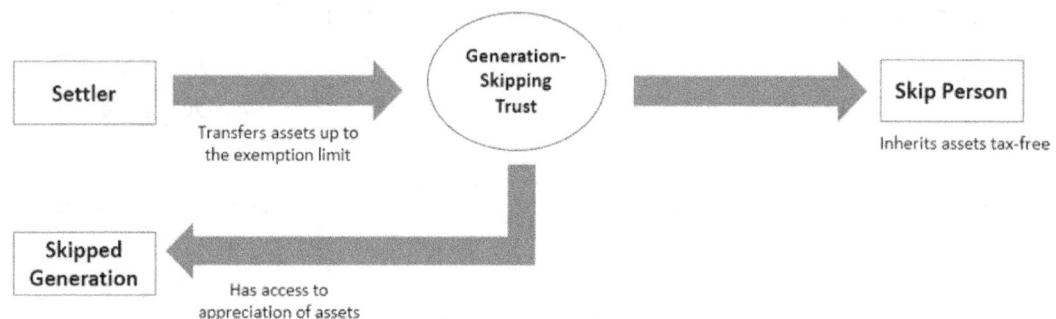

- **Grantor Retained Annuity Trust (GRAT)**: Transfers asset appreciation to beneficiaries while retaining a fixed annuity payment for a term, thus minimizing gift taxes. Advantages include the potential to transfer substantial growth out of the estate and providing a steady income stream for the grantor. Disadvantages include the risk if the grantor dies during the term and the dependence on asset performance, which can be unpredictable.

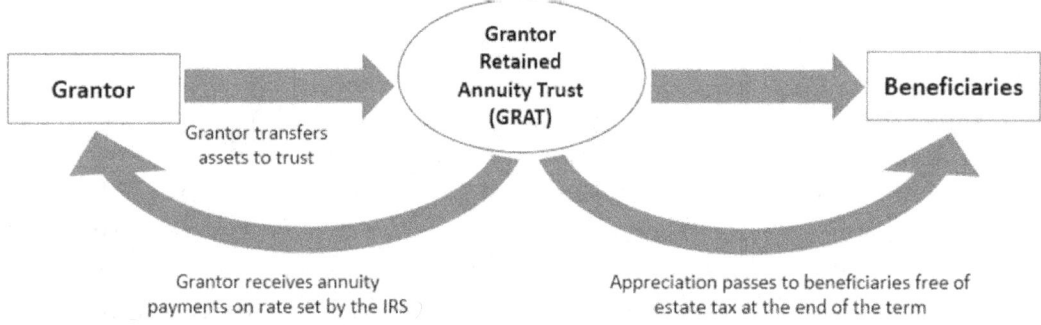

- **Marital Trust**: Benefits the surviving spouse, often used in second marriages to balance interests between the surviving spouse and children from a previous marriage. Advantages are financial support for the surviving spouse and balancing different family interests. Disadvantages include potential estate taxes on the surviving spouse's estate and complexities in managing family dynamics.

- **Charitable Remainder Trusts (CRTs)**: CRTs are irrevocable trusts that provide an income stream to the donor or beneficiaries for a term, with the remainder going to charity. They're ideal for converting appreciated assets into income, offering tax deductions, and supporting charitable causes.

    o *Charitable Remainder Annuity Trust (CRAT)*: A CRAT distributes a fixed annuity payment annually, offering predictable income. It suits donors seeking stability in their charitable contributions and financial returns.

    o *Charitable Remainder Unitrust (CRUT)*: Unlike a CRAT, a CRUT pays a fixed percentage of the trust's assets, recalculated annually. This allows for potential income growth if the trust's assets increase in value.

    o *Flip-CRUT*: Designed for assets that might not initially produce income (like real estate), a Flip-CRUT starts as a CRUT but 'flips' into a standard unitrust upon a triggering event, like the sale of the asset. This flexibility makes it attractive for

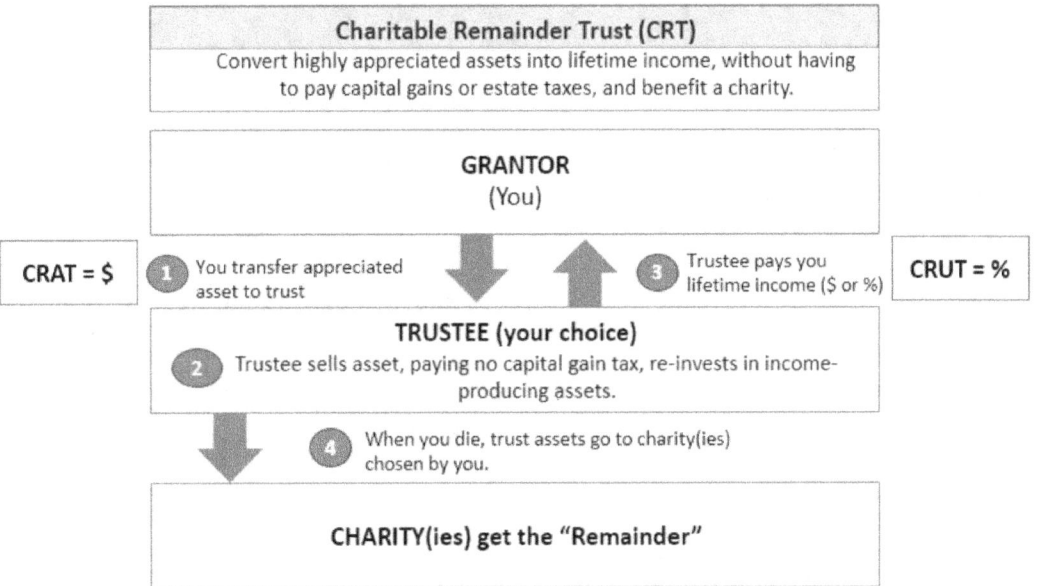

    o *Charitable Lead Trusts (CLTs)*: CLTs benefit charitable organizations first with an income stream for a set term, after which the remainder passes to the donor's heirs. They are an excellent way to fulfill immediate philanthropic goals while ensuring wealth transfer to the next generation with potential tax advantages.

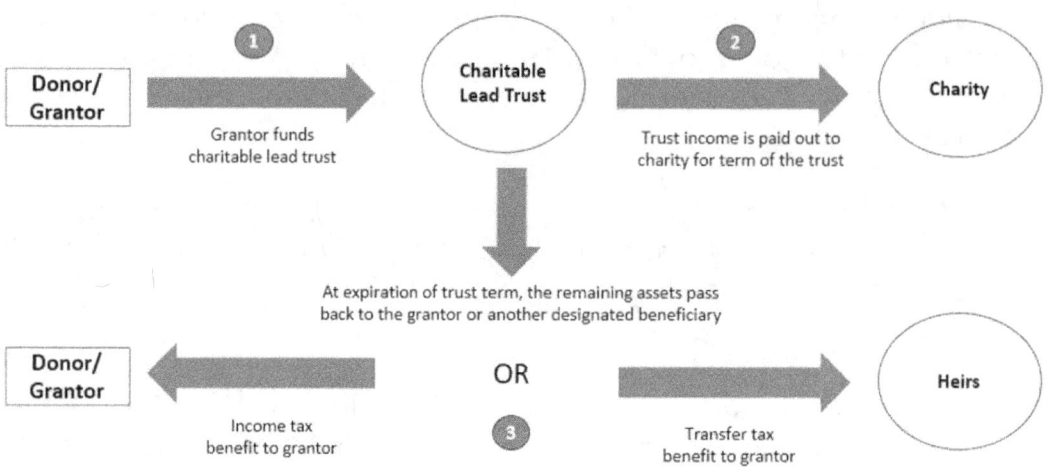

- **Qualified Terminable Interest Property Trust (QTIP)**: Provides income to a surviving spouse while preserving the principal for other beneficiaries. Advantages include ensuring support for the surviving spouse with income and controlling the final distribution of assets. Disadvantages are the limited access to the principal for the surviving spouse and the necessity for precise drafting.

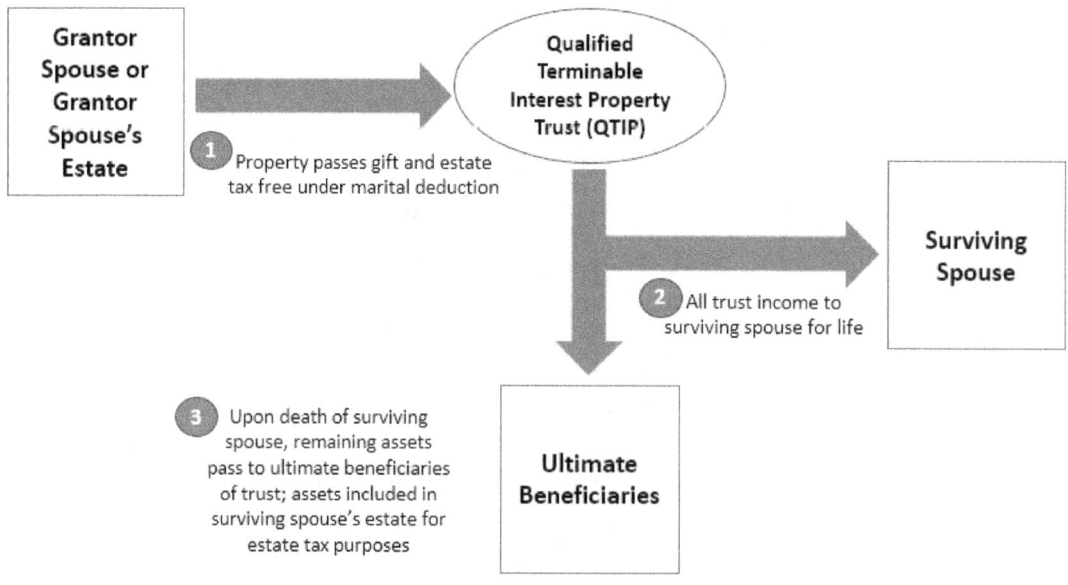

- **Testamentary Trust**: Established through a will and activated upon the grantor's death, for such purposes as managing assets for beneficiaries like minors. Advantages include being tailored to specific beneficiary needs and offering posthumous control over asset distribution. Disadvantages are subjecting the trust to probate, potentially delaying asset distribution, and the lack of flexibility post-creation.

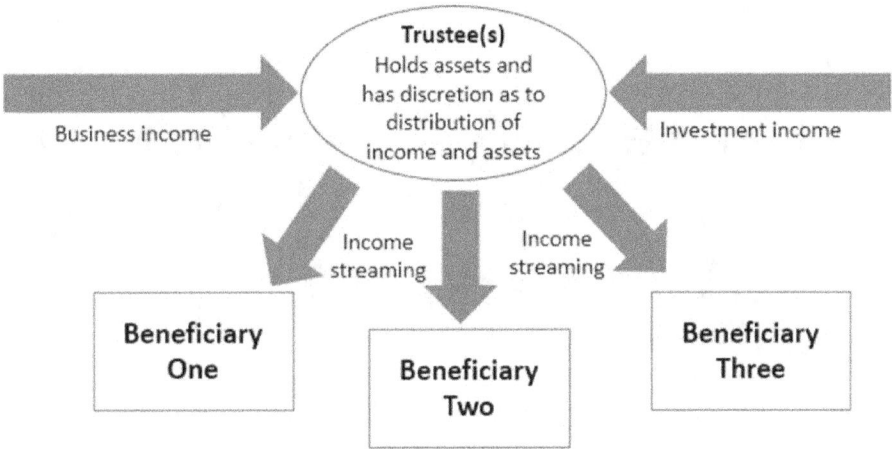

- **Special Needs Trust**: Provides for a beneficiary with disabilities without jeopardizing their eligibility for government aid. Advantages include protecting government aid eligibility and being tailored to the beneficiary's specific needs. Disadvantages involve complex rules for maintaining eligibility and the need for careful management and oversight.

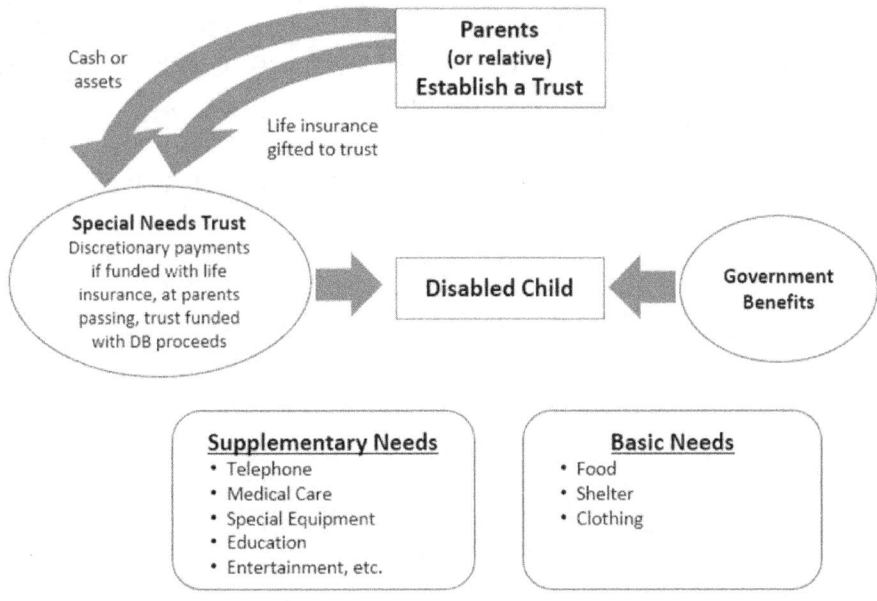

- **Irrevocable Life Insurance Trust (ILIT)**: An ILIT is a trust designed to own a life insurance policy, removing the death benefit from your taxable estate. This strategy shields the proceeds from estate taxes, providing a tax-efficient method to transfer wealth. ILITs can also offer control over the distribution of proceeds, ensuring that the benefits are used in line with the grantor's wishes, such as paying estate taxes, debts, or providing income to beneficiaries.

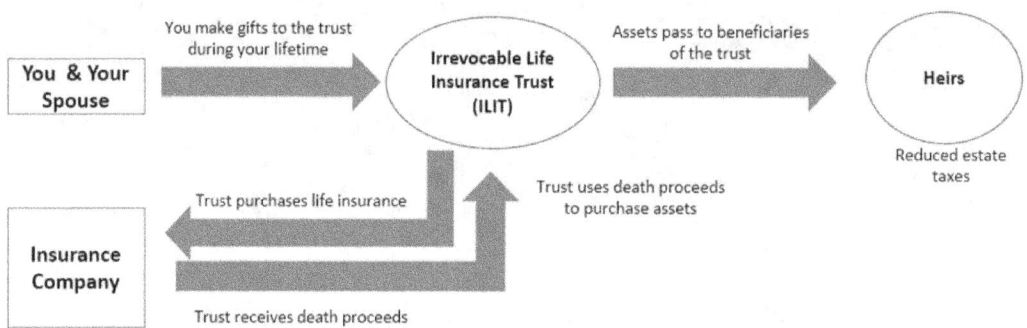

- **7702 Plan**: Under the Internal Revenue Code Section 7702, life insurance policies that comply with certain cash value accumulation tests offer tax-advantaged benefits. These include tax-deferred growth of cash value, tax-free loans and withdrawals under specific conditions, and tax-free death benefits. "7702 plans" often refer to policies designed to maximize these tax benefits, serving as a tool for both savings and estate liquidity.

- **Retained Life Estate**: Transferring ownership of a property to a charitable organization while retaining the right to occupy or use the property for life or a specified period. Pros; avoid probate, possible life tenant tax breaks, remainderman capital gains tax advantages. Cons; Potential effect of remainderman financial problems, effect on financing, remainderman's heirs if remainderman dies first, Medicaid impact.

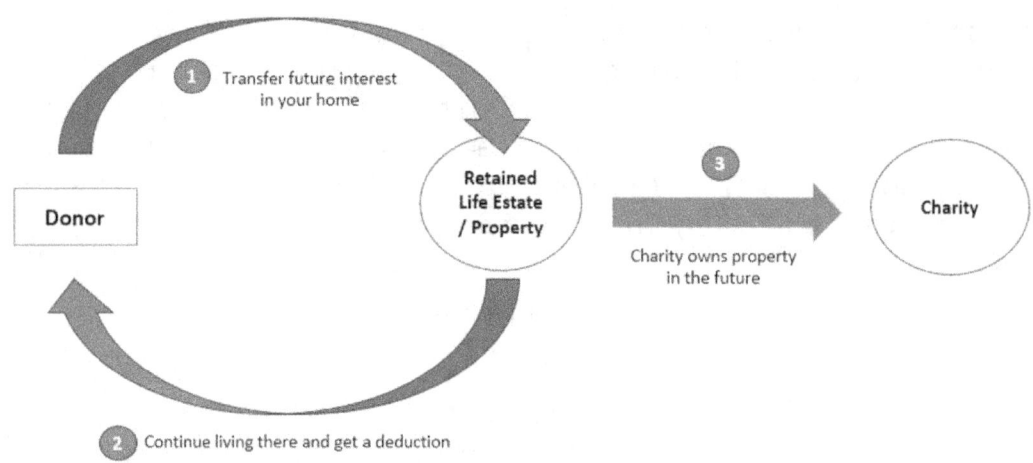

- **Indexed Universal Life (IUL) Insurance**: IUL policies offer flexible premiums and death benefits with a cash value tied to a stock market index, such as the S&P 500, but with protective features against market downturns. IULs can be an attractive option for those seeking the potential for cash value growth while maintaining a death benefit. The cash value can be accessed via loans or withdrawals, offering financial flexibility for estate planning needs.

Indexed Universal Life Insurance	vs.	IRA and 401(k)
Contracts protect against losses while offering some equity risk premium		Does not offer the same downside, though there is no cap on returns
Complicated policies and excessively high fees that eat away at returns significantly over time		Fees are lower than those that come with a IUL
Best for high net worth individuals looking to reduce their taxes		Contributions accrue tax-free, but taxes are taken out when money is withdrawn

- **Disclaimer Trust**: Allows beneficiaries, usually the surviving spouse, to decline part or all of the inheritance, with disclaimed assets passing into a trust. Advantages include post-death flexibility for estate planning and potential tax advantages. Disadvantages are the necessity for a timely, irrevocable decision by the beneficiary and the complexity in understanding and executing the disclaimer process.

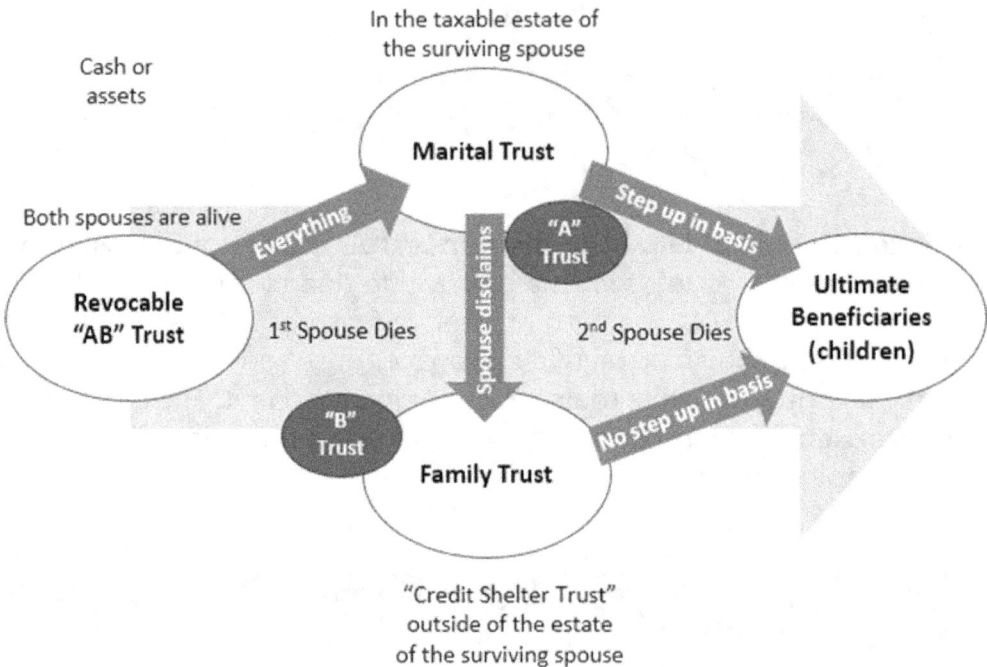

- **Qualified Terminable Interest Property Trust (QTIP)**: Provides income to a surviving spouse while preserving the principal for other beneficiaries. Advantages include ensuring support for the surviving spouse with income and controlling the final distribution of assets. Disadvantages are the limited access to the principal for the surviving spouse and the necessity for precise drafting.

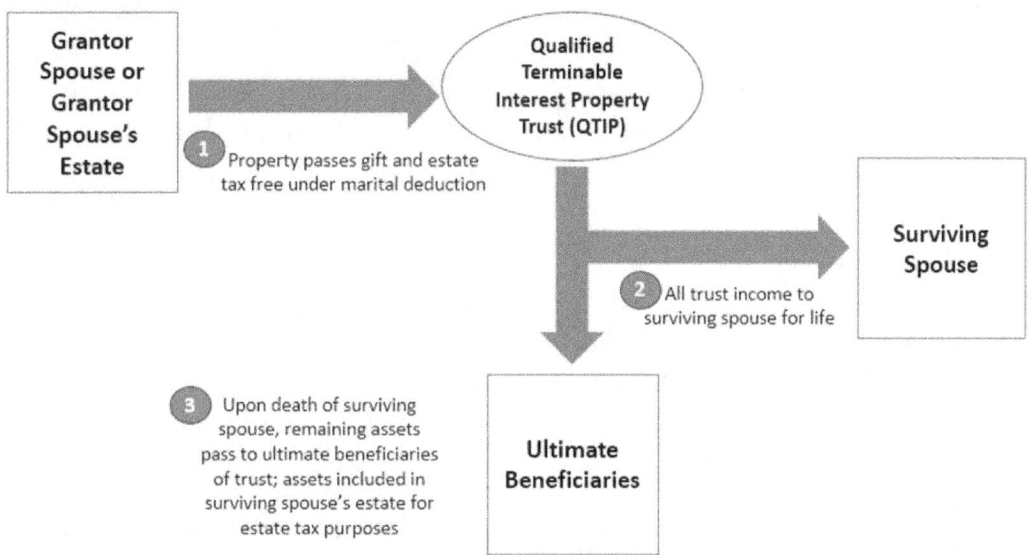

- **Intentionally Defective Irrevocable Trust (IDIT)**: An irrevocable trust with a flaw, allowing the grantor to pay income taxes on trust assets, thereby reducing the estate size for tax purposes. Advantages are its efficiency in transferring appreciating assets to beneficiaries and in reducing the taxable estate. Disadvantages include its complex structure, tax reporting requirements, and irrevocable nature.

Wills

Wills are fundamental documents in estate planning, serving as directives for asset distribution and final wishes. Here's an overview of various types of wills:

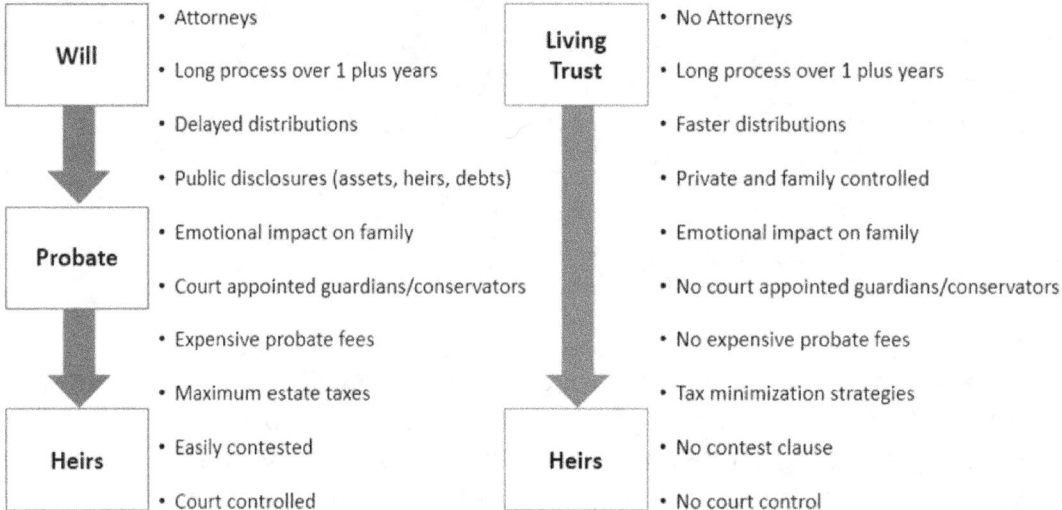

- **Living Will**: Specifies medical treatment preferences in cases of incapacity, including life-sustaining measures. Advantages include ensuring medical decisions align with personal wishes and providing clarity to family and healthcare providers. Disadvantages involve the need for regular updates to reflect current wishes and medical advancements.

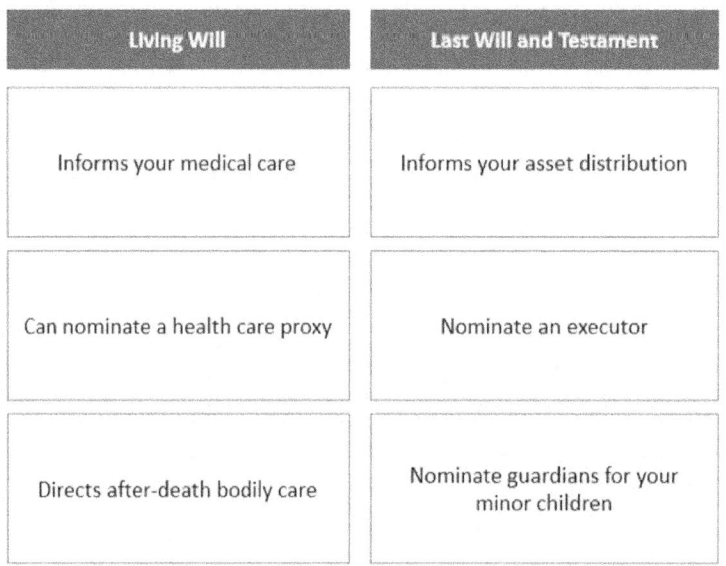

- **Simple Will**: A basic will for asset distribution, naming an executor, and potentially appointing guardians for minor children. Advantages include ease of preparation and straightforwardness, suitable for uncomplicated estates. Disadvantages are limited capability in complex estate planning and potential for probate delays and costs.

- **Joint Will**: A single will created by two people, usually spouses, that is binding on both parties. Advantages include simplicity in expressing mutual wishes and estate planning efficiency for couples. Disadvantages involve inflexibility, as changes cannot be made after the first death, and potential disputes among beneficiaries.

- **Testamentary Trust Will**: Includes provisions to create a trust upon the testator's death for asset management. Advantages include posthumous control over asset distribution and potential protection for minors or special needs beneficiaries. Disadvantages are the complexity of drafting, potential probate delays, and the fixed nature of the trust provisions.

- **Holographic Will**: Entirely handwritten and signed by the testator, potentially without witnesses. Advantages include personalization and no need for legal formalities or witnesses. Disadvantages involve risks of being deemed invalid due to non-compliance with state laws and lack of legal guidance in drafting.

- **Mirror Will**: Separate wills by two people, usually spouses, where each will mirrors the other's terms. Advantages include reflecting each other's wishes and simplicity in estate planning for couples. Disadvantages are potential challenges if circumstances change and one party wants to alter their will independently.

- **Nuncupative Will**: An oral will made under imminent threat of death, limited in scope and legal standing. Advantages include conveying last wishes in urgent situations. Disadvantages involve limited legal recognition, limited scope, and reliance on witness testimonies, which may lead to disputes.

- **Pour-Over Will**: Directs assets not in a trust at death to be transferred to a trust, complementing trust planning. Advantages include ensuring all assets are eventually managed within a trust structure and simplifying estate administration. Disadvantages involve the requirement of probate for the pour-over assets and the necessity of an existing trust.

Other Common Tools

Beyond trusts and wills, other tools are vital for comprehensive estate planning. Here's a closer look at these tools:

- **Health Care Directive**: Outlines preferences for medical care in scenarios where decision-making capability is lost. Advantages include ensuring medical decisions reflect personal wishes and providing clear instructions to healthcare providers. Disadvantages involve the need for regular updates to reflect current health preferences and potential challenges in interpreting the directive.

California Advanced Health Care Directive

Part 1: Choose a medical decision maker.
A medical decision maker is a person who can make health care decisions for you if you are too sick to make them for yourself.

Part 2: Make your own health care choices.
This form lets you choose the kind of health care you want. This way, those who care for you will not have to guess what you want if you are too sick to tell them yourself.

Part 3: Sign the form.
The form must be signed to be used.

- **Beneficiary Designations**: Direct transfer of certain assets like retirement accounts and life insurance to specified beneficiaries. Advantages include bypassing probate and providing a straightforward transfer of assets. Disadvantages are potential outdated designations if not regularly reviewed and lack of flexibility once the beneficiary is designated.

- **Joint Tenancy with Right of Survivorship**: Co-ownership where property passes automatically to surviving owners, bypassing probate. Advantages include simplicity in transfer upon death and avoiding probate.

Disadvantages involve lack of estate planning flexibility and potential issues if relationships change.

- **Tenancy by the Entirety**: Joint ownership for married couples, offering protection from individual debts. Advantages include asset protection from individual creditors and automatic transfer to the surviving spouse. Disadvantages are that it is limited to married couples and potential complications may arise in case of divorce.

- **Community Property with Right of Survivorship**: Joint ownership for married couples in community property states, allowing property to pass to the surviving spouse without probate. Advantages include simplifying transfer after death and potential tax benefits. Disadvantages are applicability limited to certain states and potential complexities in distinguishing community property.

- **Charitable Gifts**: Donating assets to charity, potentially providing tax benefits. Advantages include supporting charitable causes and potential income tax deductions. Disadvantages are the irreversible donation of assets and the need for careful planning to align with overall estate strategy.

- **Qualified charitable distributions (QCDs)**: Those who are 70½ or older and those that are required to take minimum distributions from their IRA accounts can use a qualified charitable distribution to help meet this requirement.

    o The distribution from your IRA will go directly to a charity of your choosing
    o You can give up to $100,000 annually
    o The SECURE 2.0 allows for one-time election to gift $50,000 to Gift Annuity or Charitable Remainder Trust
    o You may avoid taxes on your IRA distributions

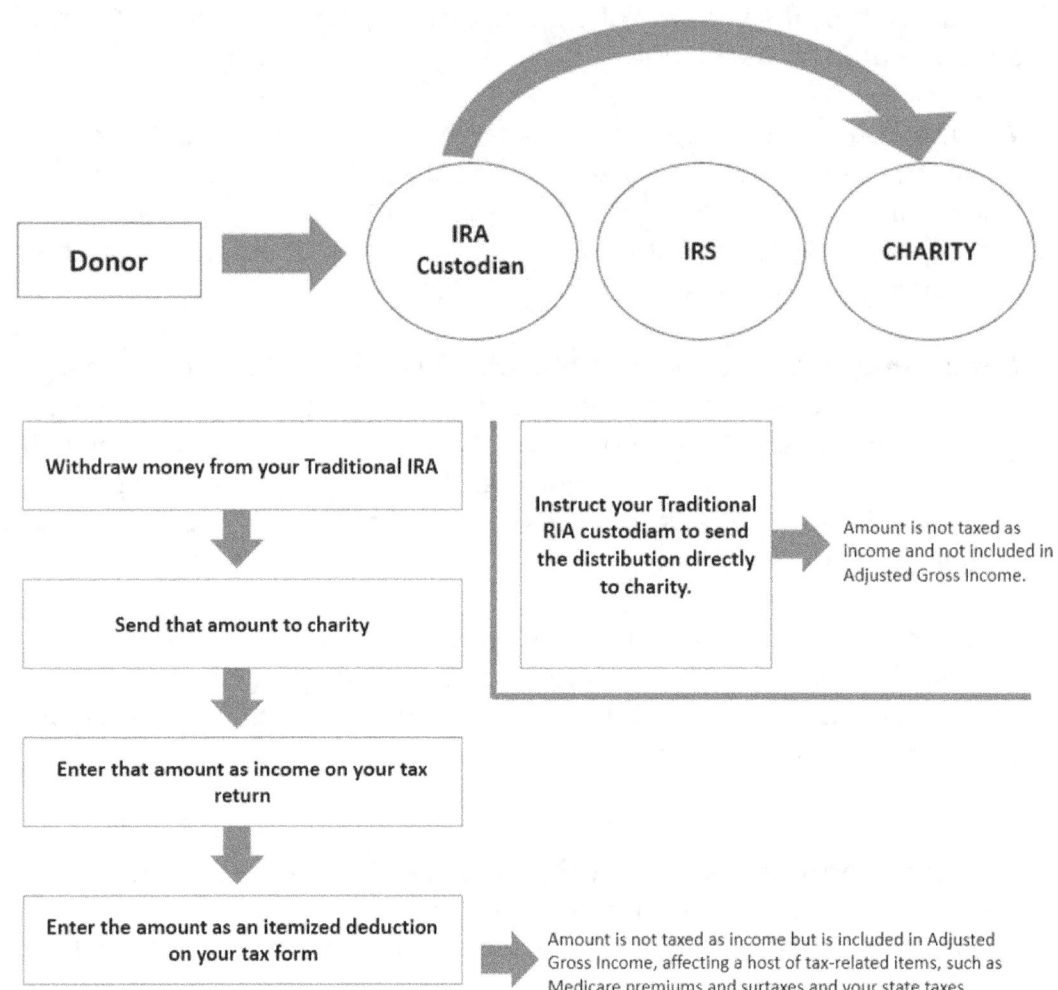

- **Gifting of Assets**: Transferring assets to others during life, which can reduce the taxable estate. Advantages include reducing estate size for tax purposes and the joy of seeing beneficiaries use the gifts. Disadvantages are potential gift tax implications and the loss of control over the gifted assets.

- **Donor-Advised Funds (DAFs)** have increasingly become a cornerstone of strategic philanthropy, offering a blend of simplicity, flexibility, and tax efficiency that appeals to a wide range of donors. By allowing individuals to make charitable contributions and receive immediate tax deductions, all while advising on the distribution of funds at a later date, DAFs represent a pivotal tool in modern charitable planning. This section will explore DAFs in the context of broader philanthropic strategies, including life estates, beneficiary designations, life insurance, and qualified charitable distributions, comparing their benefits and limitations to those of private foundations.

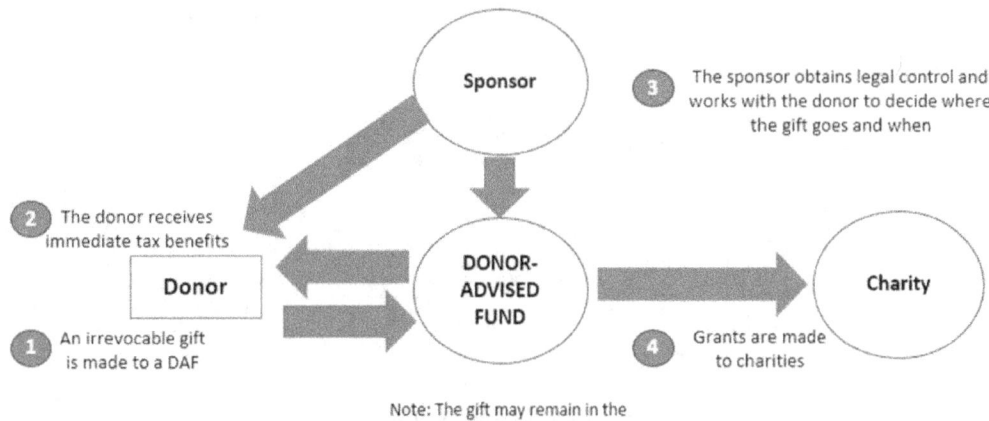

- **Letters of Instruction**: Informal documents providing guidance for estate management and distribution. Advantages include offering clear, personal instructions to executors and beneficiaries. Disadvantages are their non-legally binding nature and potential for being overlooked or misunderstood.

- **Power of Attorney**: Legal authority granted to someone to act on your behalf in various matters. Advantages include ensuring decisions are made by a trusted individual if you're unable. Disadvantages are potential abuse of power and the need for absolute trust in the appointed person.

Types of Power of Attorney	USE	MOST USEFUL FOR
Durable Power of Attorney	Can be used whether the Principal is incapacitated or not.	Estate planning and delegating your financial affairs.
Springing Power of Attorney	Activates on a future date or when a specified event occurs.	Planning for your incapacity or absence.
Special Power of Attorney	Allows an Agent to perform only one or two specific duties.	• Delegating tasks to experts (such as realtors or brokers)
Medical Power of Attorney	Lets the Agent make medical decision for the Principal.	Planning for medical emergencies in the future.

- **Payable on Death (POD) Accounts**: Designation on accounts for direct transfer of funds to beneficiaries upon death. Advantages include easy and direct transfer of funds, bypassing probate. Disadvantages are potential disputes among beneficiaries and the need for regular updates.

- **Digital Asset Management**: Planning for the management and disposition of digital assets like online accounts. Advantages include ensuring digital assets are accounted for and properly managed after death. Disadvantages are the complexity of managing diverse digital assets and ensuring access information is up-to-date and secure.

COMMON MISTAKE ALERT: Using the wrong tool

Like using the wrong golf club, choosing an inappropriate estate planning tool can limit effectiveness. Each tool serves a specific purpose; ensure your selection aligns with your plan's goals. The wrong tool could result in having to go through the probate process - did I mention that was bad? Remember, this list isn't exhaustive. Always consult with professionals for personalized advice.

2.8 Annual Reviews; Adapting to Legal, Regulatory, and Familial Changes

The only constant in life is change, and your legacy plan should reflect this. Regular reviews ensure your plan remains relevant and effective in the face of legal changes, shifts in family dynamics, and other life events. This section will guide you through the process of reviewing and updating your plan, ensuring it evolves along with your family and the world around you.

Life's "trigger events" are significant occurrences that necessitate a review of your legacy plan. These include:

- Marriage or Divorce
- Birth or Adoption of a Child/Grandchild
- Death of a Family Member
- Retirement
- Disability
- Starting or Selling a Business
- Acquiring or Disposing of Major Assets (like property)
- Significant Changes in Financial Status
- Major Health Diagnoses
- Changes in Tax Laws

COMMON MISTAKE ALERT: Failing to spot a trigger event

In the whirlwind of life's milestones, whether joyous or challenging, it's crucial to recognize these as trigger events. Not updating your plan accordingly can lead to complications. Treat your legacy plan as a living document, evolving with your life's journey.

2.9 Business Entity Structures

When it comes to estate planning, grasping the various types of company structures and their relevance is essential. Each structure carries its own set of rules for asset distribution, tax liabilities, and business operations. We're about to delve into the world of LLCs, Corporations, and Partnerships, exploring the unique facets and strategic implications of each within the scope of estate planning.

A popular choice in this realm is the Limited Liability Company (LLC), prized for its liability protection, tax benefits, and operational flexibility. But remember, there's no one-size-fits-all solution here. The right business entity for your estate plan hinges on the specific nature of your assets, your goals, and the unique dynamics of your family.

To give you a comprehensive understanding, I've prepared detailed discussions on these common business structures, dissecting their advantages and potential pitfalls. And for those burning questions you might have, don't miss the FAQ section at the end of this chapter, dedicated exclusively to estate planning and business entities. This guide is designed to provide clarity and direction, but always remember the value of a professional's insight in these matters.

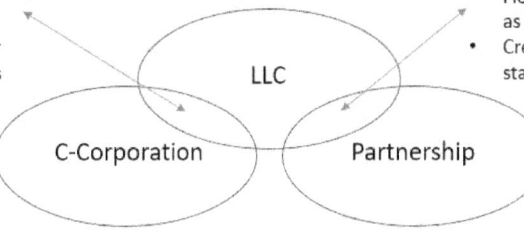

2.9 (a) LLCs (Limited Liability Companies)

- **Benefits**: LLCs offer flexibility in management and distribution of profits. They provide limited liability protection, meaning personal assets are generally protected from business debts.

- **Drawbacks**: Depending on the state, LLCs can have higher formation and maintenance costs. The transfer of membership interests in estate planning can be complex, especially if operating agreements don't clearly outline transfer procedures.

- **Common Use in Estate Planning**: LLCs are often used to hold real estate or family businesses due to their liability protection and pass-through taxation, which avoids double taxation.

2.9 (b) Corporations (S-Corps and C-Corps)

- **Benefits**: Corporations offer limited liability protection. S-Corps have pass-through taxation (avoiding double taxation), while C-Corps have potential tax benefits such as deductible business expenses.

- **Drawbacks**: Corporations, especially C-Corps, have more rigid structures and formalities, higher setup and operational costs, and potential double taxation (for C-Corps).

- **Common Use in Estate Planning**: Often used for larger businesses or those planning to raise capital publicly. S-Corps are favored for smaller businesses that want corporate structure with pass-through taxation.

2.9 (c) Partnerships (General and Limited)

- **Benefits**: General Partnerships are easy to form with minimal formalities. Limited Partnerships protect limited partners' personal assets from business liabilities.

- **Drawbacks**: General partners in General Partnerships have unlimited liability. Limited Partnerships require at least one general partner with unlimited liability.

- **Common Use in Estate Planning**: Suitable for family businesses where control can be centralized among a few while providing limited liability for others.

Issues and Considerations:

- **Operating and Tax Rules**: Each entity comes with its own set of rules for operation and taxation. Ignorance of these rules can lead to legal and financial complications.

- **Tax Implications on Ownership**: In entities like S-Corps and LLCs, owners can be taxed on income regardless of distributions. Owners need to understand their tax obligations, especially if the business requires cash for operations and doesn't distribute profits regularly.

- **Complexity for W-2 Employees**: New business owners, especially those used to being traditional employees, may find navigating business taxes challenging. The need to file taxes quarterly and dealing with K-1 income (a tax document that reports share of income in partnerships and S-Corps) can be daunting.

- **Unintended Consequences**: Beneficiaries who inherit business interests may find themselves with unexpected responsibilities and liabilities. They might have to engage with partners they didn't choose and deal with business dynamics they're not prepared for.

- **Professional Assistance**: It's advisable for new business owners to hire a tax professional familiar with business taxation to navigate these complexities.

Additional Considerations:

- **Business Continuity Planning**: Clear plans should be in place for the continuity or sale of the business upon the owner's death.

- **Succession Planning**: Especially important in family businesses to avoid conflicts and ensure smooth transition.

- **Estate Tax Implications**: Depending on the structure, the value of the business interest in the estate could significantly impact estate tax liabilities.

- **Buy-Sell Agreements**: These agreements can be crucial in determining how business interests are handled upon an owner's death.

In conclusion, while owning a business entity can offer benefits like asset protection and tax flexibility, it also brings complexity, especially when integrated into estate planning. Thorough understanding, professional advice, and careful planning are essential to navigate these waters effectively.

2.10 Modern Challenges (Digital Assets & Technological Advancements)

In the maze of modern estate planning, it's essential to recognize that we're navigating a digital renaissance. Our assets have expanded into the virtual sphere, and the legalities of managing them are continuously evolving. At first, like many, I approached this digital transformation with a degree of skepticism. Yet, I soon recognized the immense value these innovations offer, from delivering personalized updates on my interests to enhancing both daily life and business operations. The march of technology is inexorable, and it underscores the critical need for adaptability and open-mindedness in leveraging these developments for our benefit.

Let's explore the modern challenges that shape today's estate planning:

- **Digital Assets**: These are not just the social media accounts where we share our lives, but also encompass digital currencies and the myriad of online accounts that define our financial and personal identities.

- **Technological Advancements**: We must adapt to novel methods of managing and transferring assets, as these will undoubtedly become the norm in the near future.

COMMON MISTAKE ALERT: Not keeping pace with technology

In our rapidly advancing digital age, neglecting to stay informed can create significant blind spots in your estate plan. You don't need to be a Silicon Valley guru, but it's either up to you to keep abreast of technological changes or to ensure that your chosen successor trustee can navigate these waters adeptly. If they lack this proficiency, it may be time to reevaluate your choice to safeguard your digital legacy effectively.

COMMON MISTAKE ALERT: Neglecting digital assets

In the digital age, our lives straddle the line between the tangible and the virtual. To disregard the management of digital assets is to leave a critical component of your estate exposed. These assets are the indelible marks we leave on the digital world, encapsulating everything from our social interactions to our financial transactions.

The Solution: Your estate plan must be comprehensive, embracing both physical and digital elements. Appoint a Digital Executor who is competent in the digital domain and whom you trust to fulfill your digital asset directives. This person will be your champion in the virtual arena, managing everything from email accounts to digital photo albums and beyond. Clear, concise instructions and access to the necessary digital keys are as crucial here as they are for your physical assets. By ensuring these measures are in place, you anchor your digital legacy with the same care and intention as the rest of your estate.

2.11 Letters of Instruction

Playing poker is a lot like navigating estate planning. It's all about making the best out of the hand you're dealt, combining what you know with what you can't see. In poker, you factor in player history, position, chip counts, and more. In planning, it's about providing as much information as possible to those stepping into your shoes. Enter the Letter of Instruction – your playbook for successors. It's where you lay out all the details they'll need. This foresight, like a well-played poker hand, can prevent headaches and ensure a smooth process later on. Trust me, it's a winning move.

When it comes to estate planning, think of a Letter of Instruction as your ultimate cheat sheet. It's not just a list of assets and debts; it's the key to making sure nothing gets missed. This letter is where you detail everything from the location of your assets to how they're owned. It's like having a detailed map in a treasure hunt - except the treasure is your life's work. And the best part? Unlike a will, which can feel like its etched in stone, this letter is a living document. It's easy to update, whether it's a quick note or a comprehensive inventory, and it's a way to make sure your executor, or whoever steps into your shoes, isn't left playing a guessing game. Think of it as setting them up for success, ensuring they don't overlook anything, from the obvious to the obscure.

Here's a summary of the topics for a Letter of Instruction:

- **Available Money**: Lists all accessible funds and accounts.

- **Other Securities and Real Estate**: Details properties, land, and other real estate holdings.

- **Sources of Current Income**: Enumerates various income sources like employment, pensions, or royalties.

- **Pension/Retirement Accounts and Securities**: Information on retirement plans and investments like stocks and bonds.

- **Business Interests**: Details of sole proprietorships, partnerships, LLCs, corporations, etc.

- **Home Inventory/Valuables**: Lists valuable household items and collectibles.

- **Advisors (Money/Tax/Legal)**: Contact information of financial, legal, and tax advisors.

- **Insurance**: Details of various insurance policies.
- **What You Owe and Who You Owe**: Outlines debts and liabilities.

- **People/Services/Contracts**: Information about personal and household service providers.

- **Tax Records and Credit Cards**: Details of tax filings and credit card accounts.

- **What's Owed to You**: Lists receivables or items owed to the individual.

- **Personal Documents**: Contains important personal, legal, and professional documents.

- **Burglar Alarms, Locked Places/Keys**: Information on security systems and keys.

- **Personal Information**: Personal history, employment, and family background.

- **Hiding Places, Medical Information**: Details hidden assets and medical history.

- **Your Family**: Information about immediate and extended family.

- **Death Plans**: Preferences for organ donation, funeral arrangements, etc.

- **Estate Matters/Will**: Information about wills, trusts, and estate planning documents.

A Letter of Instruction is like a coach's playbook for your estate. It's versatile, adaptable, and can cover everything from your assets and debts to your personal wishes. Unlike a will, it can be informal and easily accessible, making sure your post-death wishes, especially about your funeral and other personal messages, are known right away. Think of it as a detailed manual for your life's admin: from when to service the car, to who trims the lawn. It's a practical guide that eases the load on your loved ones, covering the essentials that might seem minor but are incredibly useful during tough times. Remember, this isn't just a document; it's a thoughtful gesture to those who'll be managing your affairs when you're gone.

2.12 Impact on Beneficiary Retirement Accounts

Navigating the terrain of beneficiary decisions for retirement accounts is akin to a coach strategizing a long-term play. These accounts, often a significant part of an individual's assets, come with specific rules and implications after the account owner's demise. It's like understanding the nuances of a complex game plan.

Once you're 72 years old (for those born after July 1 1949 and 73 in 2023, for those turning 72 in or after 2023, the rulebook changes for most retirement accounts, and you must begin taking required minimum distributions. These accounts, including 401(k)s and IRAs, are designed to support retirement savings through tax advantages, investment growth, and creditor protection. However, the protective shield these accounts offer tends to fall away after the owner's death, leaving heirs to navigate the spend-down requirements.

The playbook for who inherits your IRAs and 401(k)s isn't your will or trust. Instead, the beneficiary designations on these accounts are the key players, dictating the next moves posthumously. It's a strategic decision – choosing the right beneficiary is more than just naming a name; it's about aligning with your overall game plan.

In some scenarios, the MVP might be the surviving spouse, inheriting the account directly. Other times, the strategy might involve dividing the account among children, grandchildren, a charity, or alongside a spouse. If your heirs are facing creditor challenges, it might be a defensive move to leave the retirement account to a trust. However, the current tax and legal environment usually favors direct beneficiary designations, with trusts coming into play for specific, complex situations.

The solution is clear: Keep your beneficiary designations for IRAs and 401(k)s current and aligned with your estate planning goals. Just as a coach review and updates the team roster, regularly review these designations to ensure they reflect your latest strategy and intentions. This proactive approach ensures your retirement assets move according to your playbook, supporting your legacy goals.

2.13 The Importance of Balance

Striking the right balance in your financial life is akin to a gymnast performing on a high beam – it requires both precision and agility. On one hand, you want to embrace diversity in your investments, capitalizing on complex strategies to maximize returns. Yet, on the other hand, you need to tread carefully, ensuring your financial setup isn't so intricate that it leads to errors or baffles those who might have to manage it after you.

Too Complicated: Streamline Your Finances

Like a gymnast eliminating unnecessary moves to perfect their routine, simplifying your finances can bring clarity and efficiency. If you've journeyed through various jobs, chances are you've accumulated multiple retirement accounts like 401(k)s or different IRAs. Navigating through this maze of accounts can be daunting for you and your heirs. Consider consolidating these scattered accounts into a single IRA. This move not only streamlines your financial landscape but also makes it easier for your successors to manage your estate efficiently.

Not Diverse Enough: Broaden Your Investment Portfolio

Just as a balanced diet is crucial for a gymnast's health, diversification is key to a healthy investment portfolio. Ask yourself: when was the last time you reviewed your 401(k) contributions or diversified your investments? It's easy to fall into the trap of overestimating the value of your wealth or inadvertently leaving behind an outdated investment portfolio. Regularly revising your investments ensures they remain aligned with current market conditions and your estate planning goals.

You don't want your legacy to be a portfolio that has dwindled due to neglect or mismanagement. Instead, aim for a well-balanced, diversified portfolio that can withstand market fluctuations and continue to grow. Regular reviews and adjustments are essential, much like a gymnast constantly fine-tuning their routine for the perfect performance.

Remember, the goal is to create a financial plan that is as elegant and effective as a well-executed gymnastic routine - diverse enough to maximize potential, yet simple enough to be managed effectively.

2.14 Funding Your Trust

Creating a trust is like drafting a star player for your team – it's a vital move, but the player only makes a difference once they're actively participating in the game. Similarly, your trust only becomes effective when it's properly funded. Here's a playbook on how to ensure your trust is fully operational:

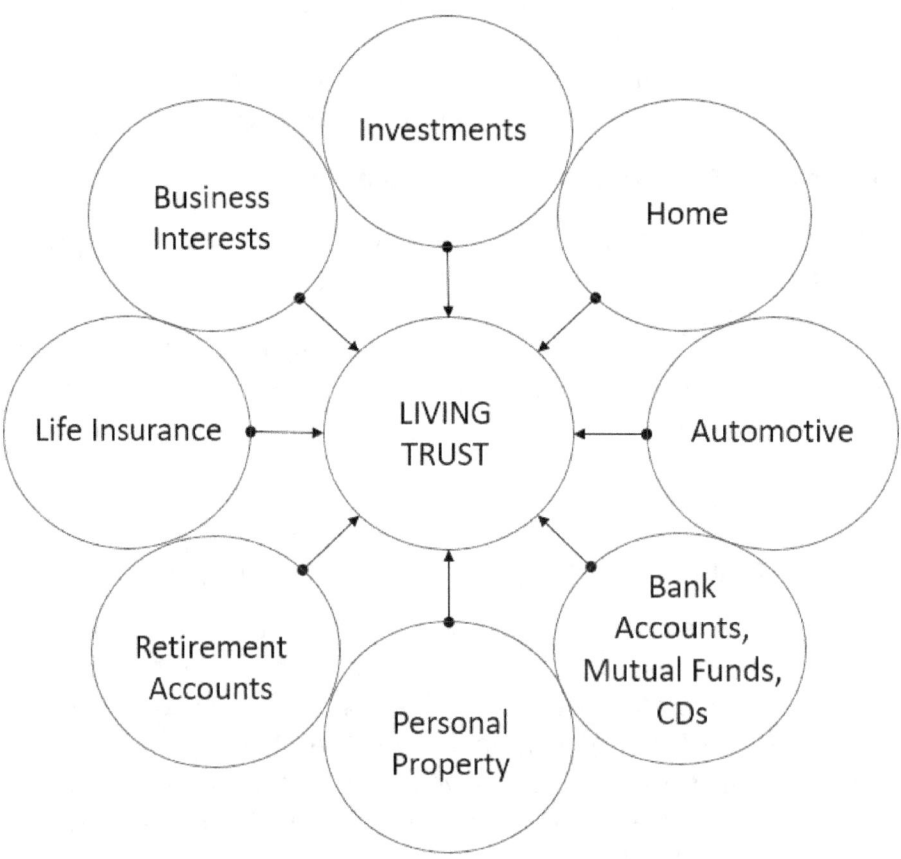

- **Title Your Assets**: This is akin to outfitting your star player in the team's uniform. Re-title your assets in the name of the trust. This includes real estate, bank accounts, and investment accounts. Consult with an attorney or financial advisor to ensure the titles align correctly with your trust's name.

- **Obtain a Taxpayer Identification Number (TIN)**: Just as a player needs a jersey number, your trust requires a TIN (note a revocable trust does not need a TIN until the grantor dies). Apply for a TIN through the IRS. This number is used to open bank accounts in the trust's name and for filing trust tax returns.

- **Personal Property and Assets Without Titles**: Think of these as the supporting team members that play a crucial role. For personal items like jewelry, art, or family heirlooms, you can assign them to your trust through a simple assignment of personal property document.

- **Assets with Titles**: These are your key players. For assets like vehicles or stocks, you'll need to change the ownership documents to reflect the trust as the new owner.

- **Real Estate**: This is your home ground advantage. To transfer real estate into your trust, you'll need to prepare and record a deed with your local county recorder's office. This process can vary, so seek professional advice.

- **Review Beneficiary Designations**: This is like ensuring your key players are in the right positions. For life insurance policies, retirement accounts, and other assets with beneficiary designations, update them to name your trust as the beneficiary, if that aligns with your estate plan.

- **Keep It Updated**: Like a team's strategy, your trust needs to adapt to changes. Regularly review and update your trust funding as your financial situation evolves.

COMMON MISTAKE ALERT: Failing to properly fund your trust

Creating a trust and leaving it unfunded is like having a playbook but never putting it into action. It's a common error that can render your trust ineffective, leading your estate directly into probate – the very scenario you intended to avoid. This oversight can cause delays, additional expenses, and potential legal hurdles for your beneficiaries. To ensure your trust operates as intended and truly reflects your legacy, commit to fully and properly funding it, just as you would commit to preparing your team for the big game.

2.15 Storing & Retrieving Your Estate Planning Documents

An expertly crafted estate plan loses its value if it's hidden away like a secret playbook that no one can find. Stashing your estate plan in a safety deposit box might seem secure, but it can become a logistical hurdle for your heirs, akin to a locked treasure chest without a key. Instead, consider storing your estate planning documents in a more accessible yet secure location, such as a fireproof safe in your home.

It's vital to inform a trusted family member, friend, or your appointed executor about the location of these documents. Remember, while digital copies are useful for reference, the original documents with your "wet" signature carry the legal weight. It's like having the official rulebook for a game – replicas might be informative, but the original is what counts in making critical decisions. So, guard it well, and ensure your loved ones know where to find it. This step is essential in making sure your well-thought-out estate plan serves its purpose effectively and doesn't become an elusive legacy.

2.16 Ensuring Estate Liquidity

One common misstep often overlooked is failing to ensure sufficient liquidity. It's akin to a team having a solid game plan but not enough resources to execute it. Liquidity, or having assets easily convertible to cash, is vital, especially when your estate needs to be divided among beneficiaries, be it children, a spouse, or others.

Imagine your estate as a complex play in a game, where each move needs to be fluid and precise. Life insurance can be an ace in your hand, providing the necessary liquidity to distribute wealth, settle debts, and maintain operations, especially if you own a business. In business scenarios, liquidity ensures that your successors have the necessary cash flow to keep the business running smoothly from day one of your absence.

For those with buy-sell agreements or business transition plans embedded in their estate strategy, maintaining liquidity is not just helpful – it's critical. Without it, these well-laid plans could falter, leaving your legacy and business in a precarious position.

Consulting with a financial advisor can help pinpoint the optimal level of liquidity for your situation. They can guide you on how to effectively create this financial buffer, ensuring your estate plan operates as intended.

Also, consider the benefits of "Transfer on Death" (TOD) designations. In many states, certain assets can get entangled in the probate court process before reaching your heirs. This process, necessary when someone dies without a will, can be both costly and time-consuming. However, assets like bank savings, CDs, and brokerage accounts can bypass this hurdle through TOD designations. This move allows your beneficiaries direct access to these assets, avoiding the complexities of probate. It's like passing the ball directly to your teammate, avoiding potential interceptions. Reach out to your bank or custodian to set up TOD designations on your accounts, ensuring a smoother transition and accessibility for your beneficiaries.

2.17 Navigating Beneficiary Designations

Managing beneficiary designations is similar to a coach ensuring the right players are in place for each play. These designations are pivotal in determining how your assets, especially those outside the will like IRAs and life insurance policies, are distributed. They need to be handled with precision and foresight, ensuring that your estate plan reflects your true intentions. Here, we explore common pitfalls and best practices in managing beneficiary designations, ensuring your estate plan scores exactly as you envisioned.

IRA Beneficiary Oversight:

- **Issue**: Failure to update IRA beneficiary designations can lead to unintended heirs receiving your assets. This occurs if the named beneficiary predeceases you or declines the inheritance, inadvertently diverting the IRA to your estate and potentially to unintended recipients.

- **Solution**: Regularly review and update your IRA beneficiary designations. This proactive step ensures your assets align with your current wishes, preventing any unintended deviations from your estate plan.

Tracking Beneficiary Designations:

- **Issue**: Inconsistent beneficiary designations across various accounts can disrupt your intended asset distribution, especially when beneficiaries are added to accounts without considering the overall estate plan.

- **Solution**: Consistently monitor and align beneficiary designations with your estate plan. Communicate specific directives to financial institutions to avoid their default rules superseding your estate wishes.

Accuracy in Naming Beneficiaries:

- **Issue**: Incorrect or outdated beneficiary names can cause delays or disputes, especially when names are not updated for suffixes, marital status changes, or legal name changes.

- **Solution**: Ensure that all beneficiary names are accurate and current, reflecting legal names as per birth certificates or official documents to prevent any confusion or legal challenges.

Naming Beneficiaries on Retirement and Insurance Accounts:

- **Issue**: Failing to name beneficiaries on retirement accounts and life insurance policies can result in these assets being distributed based on the financial institution's default rules rather than your personal wishes.

- **Solution**: Actively name beneficiaries on all retirement and insurance accounts, ensuring they align with your estate plan, as these designations can override directives in wills and trusts.

Backup Decision-Makers:

- **Issue**: Lack of contingency planning for executors and decision-makers can lead to court interventions if primary individuals are unable to fulfill their roles.

- **Solution**: Designate alternate or backup decision-makers to ensure no delays in the management of your estate and that an individual you trust will fill the role as an alternate decision-maker.

Multiple Beneficiaries and Contingent Plans:

- **Issue**: Naming only one beneficiary without contingents can create complications if the primary beneficiary is unable to inherit.

- **Solution**: Always designate more than one beneficiary, including contingent beneficiaries, to ensure seamless asset distribution according to your estate plan. This foresight ensures that your estate plan remains effective even in unforeseen circumstances, like simultaneous tragedies affecting primary beneficiaries.

By addressing these critical aspects, you fortify your estate plan, much like a coach strategizing for every possible game scenario. Ensuring that your beneficiary designations are accurate, current, and in harmony with your overall estate plan is vital to achieving your legacy goals.

2.18 Preparing Heirs: Fostering Responsibility and Independence

Navigating the process of preparing your heirs for their inheritance is akin to coaching a team for the big leagues. It's about striking the right balance between providing support and fostering independence. This section explores the intricacies of preparing your heirs, ensuring they are not only ready to receive their inheritance but also equipped to use it responsibly and constructively.

Guiding Young Heirs:

- **Child-Focused Planning**: When leaving assets to young children, it's crucial to consider their future needs and potential life paths. This involves thoughtful planning for how guardians should manage and utilize the assets for the children's benefit.

- **Avoid Restrictive Conditions**: Imposing overly restrictive conditions, like marriage or homeownership prerequisites, can lead to legal complications and asset devaluation. The key is to ensure flexibility and practicality in your stipulations.

Managing 'Problem' Beneficiaries:

- **Tailored Trust Provisions**: Addressing concerns about a beneficiary's ability to responsibly manage their inheritance calls for specific trust provisions. These can range from age-based distributions to conditions related to personal behavior, like substance abuse tests.

- **Asset Protection**: Holding the inheritance in a trust not only moderates the beneficiary's access but also offers protection from their potential creditors and life events, like divorce.

Inheritance Education:

- **Open Discussions**: Discussing inheritance with heirs can help manage expectations and prepare them for the responsibilities that come with it. It involves educating them on personal finance and introducing them to key advisors involved in your estate planning.

Promoting Financial Independence:

- **Beyond Inheritance**: Encouraging heirs to be financially independent is vital. Instilling the value of hard work and personal growth ensures they don't overly rely on the expected inheritance, which statistically is often depleted quickly.

Avoiding Overdependence on Inheritance:

- **Managing Expectations**: It's important to prevent heirs from developing an overreliance on future inheritance. This involves a balanced approach to communicating about estate plans and emphasizing the importance of personal and professional development.

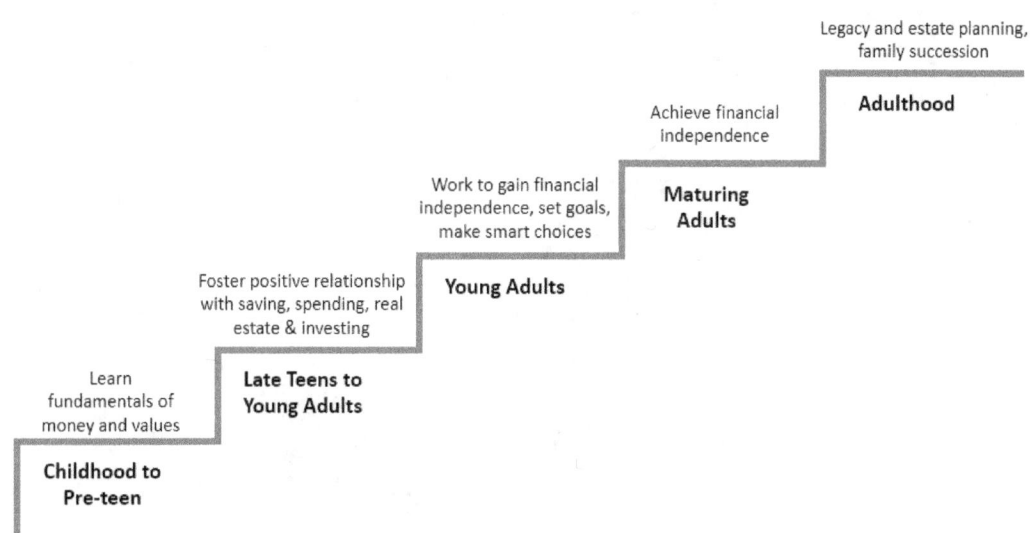

In summary, preparing your heirs for their inheritance is about more than just legal directives; it's about equipping them with the mindset and skills to handle their future responsibilities wisely. Just as a coach nurtures the talents and growth of their players, effective estate planning involves guiding your heirs to make the most of their inheritance while maintaining their independence and financial savvy.

Chapter 3

Complexities of Families – Balancing Finances with Relationships

3.1 Addressing the Challenges of Intricate Family Dynamics

3.2 Estate Planning in the Face of Cultural and Communicative Diversity

3.3 The Consequences of Overlooking the Personal Touch

3.4 Navigating Potential Familial Conflicts

3.5 The Art of Open Dialogue and Clear Communication

3.6 Maintaining Family Harmony

3.7 Contesting the Will or Trust

Chapter 3, "Complexities of Families - Balancing Finances with Relationships," is akin to a deep dive into the intricate dynamics of a sports team, focusing on the delicate balance between individual characters and the collective goal. This chapter delves into the multifaceted nature of families and the role these complexities play in estate and legacy planning.

At its core, this chapter addresses the diverse and often intricate family dynamics that can influence estate planning. Like a coach who must understand each player's unique strengths, weaknesses, and motivations, this section emphasizes the importance of recognizing and respecting the unique characteristics and needs of each family member. This understanding is crucial in preventing conflicts and ensuring that each family member's voice is heard and considered in the planning process.

The chapter also explores the impact of cultural and communicative diversity within families. Just as a sports team may comprise players from various cultural backgrounds, families today are often a blend of different cultures and communication styles. This diversity enriches the family tapestry but also adds layers of complexity to estate planning. The chapter guides readers on how to embrace these differences and integrate them into a cohesive estate plan.

An important aspect covered is the personal touch in estate planning. Beyond the financial and legal aspects, estate planning is deeply personal and emotional. This section underscores the importance of adding personal anecdotes in your estate plan and considering the emotional impact on the family. Like a team that thrives on personal connections and mutual understanding, a family's estate plan should reflect the personal values and stories that define its legacy.

Navigating familial conflicts, maintaining open dialogue, and ensuring clear communication are also key themes of this chapter. These elements are crucial for maintaining harmony and avoiding misunderstandings. The chapter likens this to a coach's role in managing team conflicts and fostering a culture of open communication and respect.

Finally, the chapter addresses the sensitive issue of contesting wills or trusts. Much like a critical play review in a sports game, contesting a will can be a complex and emotionally charged process. This section provides guidance on how to approach such situations, emphasizing the importance of fair and swift resolutions to maintain family unity and protect the estate's integrity.

Overall, Chapter 3 is a comprehensive guide to understanding and navigating the complex interplay between family relationships and estate planning. It highlights the importance of empathy, communication, and cultural sensitivity in creating an estate plan that honors and respects the unique dynamics of each family.

3.1 Addressing the Challenges of Intricate Family Dynamics

Addressing the challenges of intricate family dynamics in estate planning is essential for creating a harmonious and effective legacy. Each family possesses its unique set of dynamics and relationships, which significantly influence estate planning decisions and outcomes.

For example, in a typical family, parents might have differing views on asset distribution. One parent might prioritize equal distribution among children, while the other might consider specific needs or circumstances, like supporting a child's business venture or educational aspirations. These varying perspectives need to be reconciled thoughtfully to avoid future conflicts.

COMMON MISTAKE ALERT: Ignoring the unique needs of your family

It's common to see families where siblings have vastly different financial statuses or life choices. For instance, one child might be well-established financially, while another might struggle with financial stability. Parents need to consider how their estate plan could impact these differing situations, ensuring that it doesn't inadvertently widen gaps or create resentment.

Blended families bring another layer of complexity. Parents need to navigate the delicate balance between supporting their biological children and stepchildren. In some cases, there might be a desire to ensure that a portion of the estate is reserved for biological children while still recognizing and providing for stepchildren.

In many families, there's also the challenge of addressing the care needs of aging parents. Siblings might have different abilities or willingness to provide care, and this needs to be factored into the estate plan. It could involve setting up trusts or other mechanisms to ensure that caregiving responsibilities are acknowledged and compensated fairly.

Another common scenario involves a family member with special needs. Families need to plan for the long-term care and support of these individuals, ensuring that their inheritance is managed in a way that doesn't disrupt any governmental support they receive.

Addressing these dynamics requires open communication and a willingness to understand each family member's perspective. It's crucial to tailor the estate plan to accommodate the unique structure and needs of your family, ensuring that it reflects your values and intentions while minimizing potential conflicts and misunderstandings. This approach ensures that your estate plan is not just a financial document but a reflection of your family's unique story and relationships.

3.2 Estate Planning in the Face of Cultural and Communicative Diversity

Estate planning within culturally diverse families requires sensitive navigation and a deep understanding of differing values and traditions. Cultural diversity in families can present unique challenges in estate planning, but it also offers opportunities to create plans that are respectful and inclusive of all family members.

For instance, in a family where members have roots in different cultures, there might be varying views on inheritance, wealth distribution, and filial responsibilities. Some cultures may emphasize equal distribution among children, while others might prioritize the eldest child or sons over daughters. It's crucial to acknowledge these cultural nuances and find a middle ground that respects these perspectives while aligning with legal and ethical standards.

COMMON MISTAKE ALERT: Overlooking cultural differences

One common scenario in culturally diverse families involves differing views on healthcare and end-of-life decisions. In some cultures, there is a strong preference for aggressive medical interventions, while others may prioritize palliative care and comfort. These cultural perspectives can significantly impact decisions regarding healthcare directives and living wills.

Blended families that bring together different cultural backgrounds might also face challenges in aligning estate planning goals. There may be differences in how each culture views the role of stepchildren or the distribution of assets to in-laws. Open and honest discussions are essential to ensure that the estate plan reflects a fair and equitable approach that considers all family members.

Another aspect is the approach to charitable giving or philanthropy, which can vary significantly across cultures. Some family members might prioritize donations to religious organizations, while others might focus on educational or humanitarian causes. Balancing these preferences requires thoughtful consideration and sometimes creative solutions in estate planning.

In families where language barriers exist, clear communication becomes even more critical. It's important to ensure that all members understand the estate plan's details, possibly requiring translation services or culturally competent legal advice.

In summary, estate planning in culturally diverse families is not just about legal and financial decisions; it's about weaving a plan that respects and integrates cultural values and traditions. It requires sensitivity, open communication, and often, the guidance of professionals who understand the cultural dynamics at play. This approach ensures that the estate plan is not only legally sound but also a true reflection of the family's rich cultural tapestry.

3.3 The Consequences of Overlooking the Personal Touch

Estate planning transcends the realm of legal formalities and asset distribution; it's a journey into personalizing your legacy. It's about infusing your unique identity, your values, and your life story into your plan. This personalized approach ensures your legacy is remembered and cherished in the way you envision.

A more personal dimension in estate planning can be achieved through creative means of communication. For instance, leaving behind a heartfelt video message or a handwritten letter can provide a deeply touching and memorable experience for your loved ones. Such gestures offer comfort and a sense of closeness, making the legacy more about the individual's essence and less about material possessions.

COMMON MISTAKE ALERT: Forgetting emotional aspects.

Neglecting the emotional aspects of estate planning can lead to a plan that feels cold and impersonal. It's crucial to consider how to incorporate elements that reflect your personality, your passions, and your life experiences. This might involve including special heirlooms with sentimental value, sharing stories behind certain assets, or making specific bequests that hold personal significance.

Documenting the small, yet meaningful aspects of your life can also have a significant impact. Recording details like your favorite songs, books, recipes, or holiday traditions can keep your memory alive in the hearts of your family. These personal touches can be especially comforting during the grieving process, providing a tangible connection to you.

For those interested in leaving a more comprehensive legacy, maintaining a diary or journal can serve as a valuable tool. This can be a space to jot down your thoughts, aspirations, and life lessons – a legacy of wisdom for future generations. This practice not only allows you to reflect on your life journey but also provides your loved ones with insights into your beliefs and values.

In summary, the inclusion of personal touches in your estate plan is about more than just deciding who gets what. It's about leaving a part of yourself behind, a legacy that captures the essence of who you are. This approach can turn a legal document into a cherished keepsake, a true reflection of your life and love for your family.

3.4 Navigating Potential Familial Conflicts

Ignoring potential areas of conflict in estate planning is like a coach overlooking tensions within the team. This oversight can lead to unresolved issues festering, eventually erupting into larger disputes. It's crucial to recognize and address these flashpoints proactively:

- **Open Dialogue**: Encourage honest and open communication among family members. This can be facilitated through family meetings where everyone is given a chance to voice their opinions and concerns in a respectful environment.

- **Seek Professional Mediation**: In cases where conflicts are deeply rooted or complex, seeking the help of a professional mediator can be beneficial. Mediators can provide an impartial perspective and help guide the family towards a resolution.

- **Flexible Mindset:** Be open to understanding different perspectives and to changing your own views if necessary. This flexibility can lead to more harmonious solutions that are acceptable to all parties involved.

- **Documenting Agreements:** Once a resolution is reached, it should be documented clearly in the estate plan. This ensures that there is no ambiguity about the decisions made and the reasons behind them.

- **Regular Reviews and Updates**: As family dynamics evolve, so should the estate plan. Regularly reviewing and updating the plan in light of new developments or changes in relationships can prevent future conflicts.

By addressing conflicts head-on and fostering a culture of open communication and understanding, you can ensure that your estate plan not only reflects your wishes but also contributes to the long-term harmony and unity of your family.

COMMON MISTAKE ALERT: Ignoring conflict flashpoints

Address conflicts proactively. Effective communication and conflict resolution are key. Ignoring issues only delays them. Have the courage to tackle these matters head-on today, rather than leaving them for your heirs to resolve tomorrow.

3.5 The Art of Open Dialogue and Clear Communication

A common pitfall in estate planning is assuming that communicating something once is enough. This approach often leads to misinterpretations and forgotten details:

- **Repetitive Communication**: Reiterate important points multiple times and in different settings. Repeating key information helps reinforce it, making it more likely to be remembered and understood.

- **Diverse Communication Methods**: Utilize various methods of communication – written, verbal, and visual – to cater to different learning and comprehension styles among family members.

- **Safe and Open Environment**: Foster an atmosphere where family members feel comfortable asking questions and expressing concerns. This open dialogue can clarify doubts and strengthen mutual understanding.

- **Regular Updates and Reviews**: Estate plans should be discussed and reviewed regularly, especially after significant life events or changes in family dynamics. This practice ensures that everyone is updated and any new concerns are addressed promptly.

- **Document Important Conversations**: Keep a record of significant discussions and decisions. This can be helpful for future reference and ensures that the rationale behind certain decisions is documented.

By embracing the art of clear and open communication, you lay the groundwork for a harmonious and effective execution of your estate plan. This approach not only ensures that your wishes are understood and respected but also helps maintain family unity and trust throughout the estate planning process.

COMMON MISTAKE ALERT: Saying something only one time and in one way

There is an advertising saying that goes something like, if you are only going to do something once, you might as well not do it at all. Research on memory consolidation suggests that it may take several repetitions or exposures to information over days, weeks, or even months to move it from short-term memory into long-term memory, where it can be more easily recalled. This will be very important especially around the time your loved one nears death or shortly after. Remembering their wishes accurately is difficult under normal circumstances, when you add the stress and grief of going through an end of live event, it is made even more difficult.

3.6 Maintaining Family Harmony

Maintaining family harmony during estate planning is a delicate balancing act, similar to managing a diverse team where each member brings unique goals and perspectives to the table. It involves understanding and accommodating the different viewpoints and interests within the family. The choice of your successor trustee plays a pivotal role in this balance.

COMMON MISTAKE ALERT: Overlooking family harmony

Neglecting the importance of family harmony can lead to discord and conflict:

- **Empathetic Approach**: The successor trustee needs to demonstrate empathy and a willingness to listen to all family members. Understanding each person's perspective is crucial for maintaining harmony.

- **Balancing Interests**: It's essential to balance individual interests against the collective goals of the family. This balance helps in making decisions that are fair and considerate of everyone's needs and expectations.

- **Promote Open Dialogue**: Encourage family members to express their views and concerns openly. This openness can prevent misunderstandings and build trust among family members.

- **Consider the Bigger Picture**: Remember that family harmony often has a more lasting impact than individual gains. Decisions should be made with the long-term unity and well-being of the family in mind.

- **Seek Professional Guidance**: Sometimes, it may be beneficial to involve a neutral third-party, like a family counselor or mediator, to help navigate complex family dynamics.

- **Prioritize Health and Well-being**: Recognize that discord within the family can have adverse effects on both financial stability and personal health. Strive to make choices that foster peace and well-being.

By prioritizing family harmony in your estate planning, you not only ensure a smoother transition of your legacy but also help in nurturing and preserving family relationships. This approach underscores the importance of empathy, communication, and fairness in creating a legacy that transcends material wealth and fosters lasting familial bonds.

3.7 Contesting the Will or Trust

In the realm of estate planning, challenges to wills and trusts are not uncommon, often arising from dissatisfied parties. These challenges can stem from various legal grounds, each requiring substantial evidence to prove. Contesting a will or trust is a serious process that can alter the distribution of an estate. As an executor or successor trustee, you may find yourself navigating through these challenges, which can be as intricate and demanding as resolving a complex puzzle. This process can be financially and emotionally taxing, potentially leading to lasting family rifts.

Common Grounds for Contesting a Will or Trust:

- **Testamentary Capacity**: Challenges based on the claim that the decedent lacked the mental capacity to understand the nature of the will or trust, their assets, and the implications of their decisions at the time of signing.

- **Mental Capacity**: Similar to testamentary capacity, this challenges the mental state of the decedent, asserting that they were not of sound mind due to illness, medication, or other factors.

- **Undue Influence**: Claims that the decedent was subjected to pressure or manipulation by someone close, which resulted in a will or trust that does not reflect their true intentions.

- **Fraud or Forgery**: Allegations that the will or trust was forged, or that the decedent was deceived into signing it, believing it to be a different document.

- **Improper Execution**: Challenges based on the will or trust not meeting legal formalities, such as insufficient witness signatures or notarization issues.

- **Insufficient Information or Clarity**: Claims that the document is vague, ambiguous, or lacks necessary details, leading to confusion and disputes over interpretation.

- **Revocation or Supersession by a Later Will or Trust**: Allegations that the contested will or trust was revoked or replaced by a later document.

"No Contest" Clauses:

A "No Contest Clause," or an "in terrorem clause," is a strategic provision in a will or trust designed to deter beneficiaries from contesting. This clause works like a safeguard, penalizing beneficiaries who challenge the document and lose, often by forfeiting their inheritance. It aims to prevent costly and divisive legal battles, encouraging beneficiaries to accept the document as written. However, the effectiveness and enforceability of these clauses vary by state law, and they may not always prevent challenges.

COMMON MISTAKE ALERT: Failing to anticipate will challenges can result in lengthy, costly disputes

A significant mistake in estate planning is underestimating the potential for will or trust challenges. These disputes can lead to lengthy and costly legal battles, draining estate resources and causing deep family divides. As an executor or successor trustee, striving for swift, equitable resolutions is crucial to preserve the estate's assets and maintain family harmony.

Chapter 4

Selecting Your Successor Trustee/Executor

4.1 Defining the Roles and Responsibilities of Successor Trustee and Executor

    (a) Assembling the Trust Assets

    (b) Collecting Receivables

    (c) Valuation of the Trust Assets

    (d) Managing and Investing Trust Assets

    (e) Investing Trust Assets

    (f) Notifying The Beneficiaries

    (g) Payment of Debts, Expenses, and Taxes

    (h) Distributing Trust Assets to the Beneficiaries

    (i) Final Accounting

    (j) Duties When Death Occurs

4.2 Choosing the Right Person

    (a) Questions FOR Your Executor/Successor Trustee

    (b) Questions FROM Your Executor/Succor Trustee

4.3 Ongoing Learning in the Realm of Estate Planning

4.4 Trustee Fees and Expenses

4.5 Liabilities, Loyalties, Prudance and Protection

Chapter 4 of the book, titled "Selecting Your Successor Trustee/Executor – The Big Decision!", focuses on the significant responsibility and challenges of selecting the right individual to fulfill the dual roles of Successor Trustee and Executor in estate planning. This chapter is akin to drafting the key player in a sports team who will play a pivotal role in ensuring the successful execution of strategies and plans.

The chapter begins by defining the roles and responsibilities of successor trustees and executors. Much like a coach needs to understand each player's position on the field, this section provides a clear understanding of what each role entails. It outlines the tasks and duties associated with managing a trust and executing a will, highlighting the importance of these roles in managing and distributing an individual's assets after their death.

In choosing the right person for these roles, the chapter emphasizes the importance of careful selection, guiding the reader through the process of identifying someone who not only understands the legal and financial responsibilities involved but also aligns with the family's values and dynamics. The chapter stresses the importance of this decision, as the chosen individual will have a significant impact on how smoothly and effectively the estate plan is implemented.

The section on ongoing learning in the realm of estate planning underscores the need for continuous education and staying informed about changes in laws and regulations, much like a player who continuously hones their skills. This part of the chapter encourages both the testator and the chosen successor trustee/executor to stay abreast of the latest developments in estate planning to ensure the plan remains relevant and effective.

The discussion on trustee fees and expenses covers the financial aspects of the role. It addresses compensation and the costs associated with administering a trust or an estate, providing guidance on how to manage these aspects fairly and transparently.

Finally, the chapter delves into the liabilities, loyalties, and the principle of prudence associated with the roles of trustee and executor. This section is comparable to understanding the rules of the game and the responsibilities of upholding them. It discusses the legal and ethical obligations of these roles, emphasizing the importance of acting in the best interests of the beneficiaries and protecting the estate from potential conflicts and mismanagement.

Overall, Chapter 4 provides an in-depth guide on the critical decision of selecting a successor trustee/executor. It combines practical advice with strategic insights, ensuring that readers are well-equipped to make informed decisions in this crucial aspect of estate planning. By understanding the overlapping responsibilities and the significance of these roles, readers can approach estate planning with the confidence and knowledge necessary to make the best choices for their unique circumstances.

4.1 Defining the Roles and Responsibilities of Successor Trustee and Executor

Being a successor trustee is like being the coach and referee rolled into one. Your job is to manage the trust with a playbook handed down to you.

Time	Task	Details
Before Death		
	Locate & Confirm Estate Documents	Ensure documents are up-to-date and you have original executed versions.
	Understand Executor Duties	Research the legal duties and obligations.
	Understand Special Instructions	Anatomical gifts, body disposal, and funeral rites.
	Know the Key Contacts	Contact with key professionals, legal, tax, accounting, support, family and other.
	Gather Essential Information	Compile lists of assets, debts, account info, and key contacts.
Immediately After Death		
	Declaration of Death	Obtain and request multiple copies of the death certificate.
	Secure Property and Assets	Lock and secure all properties and assets.
	Notify Relevant Parties	Inform family, friends, and the estate attorney of the death.
	Seek Emotional Support	Reach out to counselors, clergy, or support groups.
Week One		
	Prepare Affair Documents	Organize and review necessary documents for estate planning.
	Initial Document Filing	File wills and legal documents based on attorney's advice.
	Estate Bank Account	Open a bank account for managing the estate's finances.
	Notify the Social Security Admiration and State Department of Health	Other agencies might need to be notified, check with your attorney
	Identify Trust Beneficiaries	Formal notification and waiting period could be required.
	Funeral Arrangements	Start funeral planning and coordination.
Week Two		
	Finalize Funeral Arrangements	Complete all funeral plans and payments.
	Inventory Assets	Document and appraise estate assets.
	Review Estate Finances	Assess immediate financial needs and obligations.
	Obtain Death Certificates	Ensure enough copies of the death certificate are available.
Week Three +		
	Continue Administration	Manage assets, pay bills, communicate with beneficiaries.
	Setup detailed Accounting system	Prepare and present detailed financial reports.
	Obtain trust EIN number	Seek legal and tax guidance.
	Tax Matters	File final tax returns and address estate taxes.
	Beneficiary Communication	Keep beneficiaries informed with clear, written updates.
	Notifications and Claims	Handle mail redirection, service cancellations, and file claims.
	Publishing Notice	Official publication could be required for creditors.
	Access Safety Deposit Box	Retrieve and inventory items in secure storage.
	Trust Account Transfers	Transfer assets into trust accounts as necessary into trustee name.
	Legal Challenges	Defend against any claims or actions against the estate.
	Debt Settlement	Pay off any outstanding debts.
	Asset Distribution	Distribute assets according post-probate and/or waiting period.
	Estate Closure	Complete formal estate closure after all tasks are completed.
Long-Term		
	Ongoing Communication	Regular updates to beneficiaries with good written records kept.
	Resolve Disputes	Mediate disputes and seek professional assistance if needed.
	Final or Ongoing Accounting	Provide detailed reports of all estate actions periodically.

This checklist is a general guide and the specific duties and timelines of an executor can vary based on the complexity of the estate, the laws of the state, and the particular wishes of the decedent. Executors should always consider seeking professional legal and financial advice to navigate the nuances of estate administration.

Key Responsibilities Include:

- **Scouting and Assembling Assets**: Like assembling your team, identify and gather trust assets.

- **Playing the Investment Game**: Invest these assets smartly, aiming for a balance between risk and reward.

- **The Administrative Playbook**: Handle all the behind-the-scenes work like tax filings and paying debts.

- **Distributing the Winnings**: Finally, ensure the beneficiaries receive their share as per the trust playbook.

COMMON MISTAKE ALERT: Sidestepping fiduciary duties

Ignoring your fiduciary responsibilities can lead to legal fouls. Like a coach ignoring game rules, this oversight can result in penalties.

COMMON MISTAKE ALERT: Overstepping boundaries!

Don't get reckless or careless. Mismanagement or self-dealing can land you in hot water with the beneficiaries. Remember, your playbook is the trust document, and you're playing within the field marked by state laws.

In this key section of the book, we examine the more technical aspects of being a Successor Trustee. While it's detailed and intricate, you don't need to be an expert. The goal is to provide you with a fundamental grasp of the responsibilities and guide you towards additional resources for deeper understanding. We've broken down the role into specific topics, each in its own subsection. These topics range from asset management to final accounting, ensuring you have a comprehensive roadmap for navigating the complexities of this vital role. Each subsection is numbered for easy reference and clarity.

(a) Assembling the Trust Assets
(b) Collecting Receivables
(c) Valuation of the Trust Assets
(d) Managing and Investing Trust Assets
(e) Investing Trust Assets
(f) Notifying the Beneficiaries
(g) Payment of Debts, Expenses, and Taxes

(h) Distributing Trust Assets to the Beneficiaries
(i) Final Accounting
(j) Duties When Death Occurs

4.1 (a) Assembling the Trust Assets

When you're the successor trustee, think of yourself as a detective piecing together a puzzle. Your mission? Locate all the assets entrusted to you. Here's your checklist, your treasure map if you will:

- **Real Estate:** Look for deeds or contracts that pass properties like homes, offices, or land to the trust.

- **Personal Belongings:** Check for lists or statements assigning household items to the trust.

- **Bank Accounts:** Scout for accounts listed under the trust's name.

- **Investments:** Stocks, bonds, mutual funds - if they're in the trust's name, they're yours to manage.

- **Vehicles:** Cars, bikes, boats - if the title says the trust, they're part of the haul.

- **Business Assets:** Don't miss equipment, receivables, or leases under the trust's flag.

Remember, your goal is to gather everything the trust holds, ready for the next steps of your journey.

4.1 (b) Collecting Receivables

In the role of trustee, think of yourself as a meticulous manager overseeing the trust's resources. Your task includes gathering and securing assets belonging to the trust, especially those that come into play after the trustor's passing. This involves:

- Claiming life insurance payouts where the trust is the beneficiary.
- Collecting funds from accounts like IRAs, SEPs, and 401(k)s that name the trust as the beneficiary.
- Securing other work-related benefits payable to the trust upon death.

If assets are tied up in probate, you'll need to wait for that process to conclude before adding them to the trust. Just like a seasoned coach reviewing every play, you must manage these assets with care and in line with the trust document's directives. Remember, while the court might not directly supervise this process, your duty as a trustee mirrors that of an executor, requiring the same level of diligence and integrity.

4.1 (c) Valuation of the Trust Assets

Valuating trust assets is a bit like a referee reviewing a play - crucial for fair outcomes. It's necessary for several reasons:

- **Filing Taxes**: If the total value of trust and non-trust assets exceeds a certain amount (that changes over time depending on who is making the rules in any given year), a Federal Estate Tax Return (IRS Form 706) is required.

- **State Taxes**: Some states impose taxes on assets transferred at death.

- **Cost Basis**: Determine new values for assets to minimize capital gains taxes for beneficiaries.

- **Distribution Calculations**: If assets are distributed by percentage, accurate valuations are essential.

Just like in sports, where stats and scores matter, valuating trust assets is about getting the numbers right. Think of it as a referee making sure the score reflects the game's reality. This step involves figuring out the value of everything in the trust - from real estate to stocks. It's a bit like assessing a player's worth in a trade. You might use market comparisons, get a professional appraisal, or look at stock values to nail down accurate figures. It's all about ensuring each beneficiary gets their fair share, in line with the game plan laid out in the trust. And if you're curious about the tax side of things, head over to Section 7.5 – it's a deep dive into that arena!

4.1 (d) Managing and Investing Trust Assets

As a successor trustee, you're in it for the long haul, like a coach building a dynasty. Your job isn't just to distribute assets quickly; you may need to manage them for years, even decades. Think of it as a marathon, not a sprint. You're guided by the prudent investor rule, which is like a coach's playbook for smart, long-term strategies. Your moves should be careful, focusing on stable growth and protecting the trust's principal. It's about striking a balance between scoring points (income) and defending your turf (asset preservation). Remember these three key attributes of a good manager:

- **Strategic Management:** Just like adjusting team strategies, you may need to shift or reinvest assets as market conditions change.

- **Prudent Investor Rule:** This rule is your playbook. It's about making decisions as any prudent person would in managing their own affairs, avoiding risky speculations.

- **Balancing Risk and Reward:** Diversify investments. Think of it as having a well-rounded team - some players for defense (safe investments), others for offense (higher yield but riskier).

COMMON MISTAKE ALERT: Short-sighted investments

Don't get caught up in the excitement of risky, high-reward plays. Like a coach ignoring the long-term development of the team for quick wins, imprudent investments can jeopardize the trust's future. Stay prudent, focused on the long game.

4.1 (e) Investing Trust Assets

As the team's manager, your role is to make investment plays that both guard and grow the trust's assets. Picture yourself as a coach deciding between aggressive and conservative plays. If the trust playbook (document) gives you specific investment strategies, great – follow them but still play it smart. Sometimes, you might need to call an audible and deviate from the playbook, especially when sticking to the script might hurt the team's long-term goals.

COMMON MISTAKE ALERT: Over-concentration and ignoring market changes

Don't put all your eggs in one basket. Diversify the investments. Remember, both inflation and interest rates can impact your game plan. Think of inflation like a slowly rising tide – it can erode the value of fixed-dollar investments. As for diversification, think of assembling a well-rounded team where each player brings different strengths to the field. Some assets might be the sturdy defense (safer investments), while others are your star strikers (riskier for higher yield). This strategy helps protect the trust from unexpected market shifts, ensuring a balanced and resilient team.

4.1 (f) Notifying the Beneficiaries

Being a trustee is akin to being a coach who needs to keep their team well-informed. Your duty is to communicate with beneficiaries about the trust's status, assets, and terms. Remember, each state has its own playbook when it comes to the timing and method of notifications. Avoid the pitfall of "losing on a technicality" by ensuring compliance with state-specific requirements - check with your professional team to nail this part. Missteps in communication can lead to distrust, disputes, and even legal actions against you. For more insights on effective communication and documentation strategies, see Section 7.4.

COMMON MISTAKE ALERT: Neglecting timely and accurate communication

Failing to communicate effectively with beneficiaries is like a coach who doesn't update their players on game strategies. This oversight can lead to confusion, disputes, and even legal challenges against the trustee. Stay on top of this to maintain a harmonious and transparent trust administration process.

4.1 (g) Payment of Debts, Expenses, and Taxes

As a trustee, think of yourself as a manager handling the financials of a sports team. You may not always need to notify the deceased's creditors, depending on state laws. However, if the trust or state rules demand it, creditors must be notified and debts settled. Coordination with the executor is key if there are probate assets involved. Remember, it's your job to pay the trust's bills and obligations, much like ensuring a team's expenses are covered. This includes everything from professional fees to maintaining properties or assets within the trust.

COMMON MISTAKE ALERT: Overlooking debts and expenses

Failing to manage debts and expenses properly can be like a team ignoring its financial obligations – it leads to trouble. Ensure all debts are identified and settled according to the trust terms and state laws to maintain the trust's integrity and avoid potential legal issues.

4.1 (h) Distributing Trust Assets to the Beneficiaries

When it comes to distributing the trust assets, your role shifts to ensuring that each beneficiary receives exactly what's outlined in the trust document. This part of the process mirrors the distribution steps seen in probate estates.

It's essential to have each beneficiary acknowledge their receipt of assets. If the trust consists largely of non-liquid assets, you may need to liquidate some to ensure equitable distribution. In cases where the assets include a business or partnership, direct distribution of these interests might be necessary. Open communication with beneficiaries is key to a smooth process.

COMMON MISTAKE ALERT: Inadequate or unfair distribution

Not distributing assets according to the trust document can lead to disputes and legal challenges. It's vital to adhere strictly to the instructions in the trust document and ensure each beneficiary is clear about how and what they are receiving to avoid potential conflicts.

4.1 (i) Final Accounting

Finalizing your role as a trustee involves providing a detailed final accounting to all beneficiaries. This report should encompass all income, expenses, and transactions handled by the trust up to the point of final distribution. It's a good practice, and sometimes a legal requirement, to get signed acknowledgments from beneficiaries for this final accounting. This step ensures clarity and transparency, preventing any future disputes or misunderstandings regarding the management and distribution of trust assets.

COMMON MISTAKE ALERT: Skipping final accounting

Neglecting to provide a final accounting can lead to confusion or suspicion among beneficiaries. Ensure full transparency to maintain confidence and avoid potential legal complications.

Task	Details
Notify Stakeholders	Inform all beneficiaries and relevant parties of the start of closure proceedings.
Finalize Taxes	Ensure final personal, estate, and any other tax returns are filed and taxes paid.
Complete Asset Distribution	Distribute remaining assets as per the estate plan after all debts and taxes are paid.
Close Accounts	Terminate the estate's bank accounts and cancel any outstanding subscriptions or services.
Discharge Obligations	Pay any final expenses or debts associated with the estate.
Document Review	Ensure all estate-related documents are properly filed or recorded, including deeds and titles.
Court Approval	Obtain court approval for the final accounting and distribution if required by law.
Release Liens	Ensure all liens or encumbrances on estate property are released.
Final Accounting	Provide a detailed final accounting to beneficiaries and/or the court.
Archive Records	Securely store or archive estate records for the required period according to state laws.
Obtain Receipts	Get signed receipts from beneficiaries for distributions made.
Professional Consultation	Consult with an attorney to confirm all legal requirements have been met.
Confirm Estate Plan Fulfillment	Verify all terms of the will and/or trust have been fully executed.
Notify Probate Court	Inform the court of estate completion and seek formal discharge as executor.

This checklist is a general outline and does not encompass all specific legal and financial steps required in estate closure. Executors should seek professional advice to ensure compliance with all applicable laws and regulations.

4.1 (j) Duties When Death Occurs

Embarking on the role of an executor or successor trustee can feel like navigating through uncharted territory, but remember, it's a journey you don't have to travel alone. You're not expected to be an expert in every facet of estate management. The key is to rely on your team of professionals, moving steadily and thoughtfully. Think of it as a marathon, not a sprint – pace yourself, take one step at a time, and gradually progress towards your destination. This chapter outlines the roadmap of duties, from immediate actions post-death to final accountings, guiding you through each crucial step of the process. Remember, going slow initially can actually speed up the process in the long run, as it helps avoid mistakes and ensures thoroughness. Your journey might be complex, but with careful steps and expert guidance, you'll reach the finish line effectively.

1. **Identifying, Collecting, and Protecting Probate Assets**: Gathering and securing the deceased's assets.
Mistake: Overlooking assets can result in incomplete distribution.

2. **Managing Real Estate, Securities, or Ongoing Business**: Overseeing assets until their final resolution.
Mistake: Poor management can lead to reduced asset value.

3. **Notifying Creditors**: Informing creditors to submit claims.
Mistake: Missing creditors might lead to legal complications later.

4. **Filing Tax Returns**: Submitting necessary tax documentation.
Mistake: Incorrect or late filing can incur penalties.

5. **Paying Debts, Taxes, and Expenses**: Settling obligations of the estate.
Mistake: Overlooking debts can result in legal challenges.

6. **Distributing Remaining Assets**: Allocating assets as per the will or laws.
Mistake: Incorrect distribution can lead to disputes among beneficiaries.

7. **Notifying the Post Office**: Redirecting mail to executor.
Mistake: Missing crucial documents or notices.

8. **Searching for Assets**: Finding all assets, including those in safe-deposit boxes.
Mistake: Overlooking assets can result in incomplete estate settlement.

9. **Inspecting and Securing Real Estate**: Ensuring property is safe and maintained.
Mistake: Neglect can lead to property damage.

10. Filing Claims for Benefits: Claiming due benefits like Social Security.
Mistake: Missing out on entitled benefits.

11. Evaluating Insurance Policies: Reviewing and adjusting coverage as needed.
Mistake: Inadequate coverage can lead to losses.

12. Protecting Collectibles: Safeguarding valuable items.
Mistake: Damage or loss due to poor protection.

13. Evaluating Wrongful-Death Claims: Considering legal actions if applicable.
Mistake: Overlooking potential claims can lead to lost compensation.

14. Meeting with Stakeholders: Discussing the estate with relevant parties.
Mistake: Poor communication can lead to misunderstandings.

15. Guardianship for Minors: Ensuring care for dependents.
Mistake: Neglecting this can lead to legal issues.

16. Special Instructions for Anatomical Gifts: Fulfilling wishes for body donations.
Mistake: Failure to comply with the deceased's wishes.

17. Hiring a Lawyer: Obtaining legal representation.
Mistake: Inadequate legal advice can lead to errors.

18. Formal Probate Administration: Deciding the necessity of formal probate.
Mistake: Choosing the wrong probate process.

19. Petitioning for Executor Appointment: Officially requesting executorship.
Mistake: Delay can hinder estate settlement.

20. Obtaining Executor's Bond: Providing a financial guarantee.
Mistake: Failure to obtain can delay proceedings.

21. **Notifying Interested Parties**: Informing those involved in the estate.
Mistake: Failure to notify can lead to legal challenges.

22. **Admitting Will to Court:** Validating the will.
Mistake: A contested will can prolong settlement.

23. **Ancillary Probate Proceedings**: Managing out-of-state properties.
Mistake: Ignoring this can complicate estate distribution.

24. **Identifying Non-Probate Assets**: Recognizing assets outside of probate.
Mistake: Mismanagement of these assets.

25. **Asset Appraisal for Tax Purposes**: Valuing assets accurately.
Mistake: Inaccurate valuation can affect tax liabilities.

26. **Small Estate Procedures**: Considering simplified processes.
Mistake: Overcomplicating the process.

27. **Publishing Notice to Creditors**: Officially announcing the death.
Mistake: Failure to publish can lead to undiscovered claims.

28. **Contesting Creditors' Claims**: Challenging invalid claims.
Mistake: Accepting false claims can deplete the estate.

29. **Investment Decisions**: Managing securities.
Mistake: Poor decisions can reduce estate value.

30. **Evaluating Business Future**: Deciding on business continuation.
Mistake: Mismanagement can result in business failure.

31. **Deciding on Asset Liquidation**: Choosing which assets to sell.
Mistake: Selling assets without proper valuation.

32. **Family Allowance Payments**: Ensuring family support during probate.
Mistake: Neglecting this can cause hardship.

33. **Collecting Various Assets**: Gathering diverse assets.
Mistake: Incomplete collection affects distribution.

34. **Opening Executor's Bank Account**: Managing estate funds.
Mistake: Mismanagement leads to financial discrepancies.

35. **Inventory Filing**: Documenting all assets.
Mistake: Incomplete inventory can lead to disputes.

36. **Estimating Cash Needs**: Planning for expenses and bequests.
Mistake: Inadequate planning can lead to financial shortfalls.

37. **Final Accounting and Fee Approval**: Finalizing the estate's financial dealings.
Mistake: Inaccurate accounting lead to legal issues and delays in closing the estate.

Task	Details
Obtain Official Death Certificate	Request multiple copies for various administrative procedures.
Secure the Deceased's Property	Ensure the deceased's residence and personal property is secure.
Arrange Care for Dependents and Pets	Ensure children, elderly dependents, and pets have care.
Notify Close Family and Friends	Share the news in a respectful and considerate manner.
Select a Funeral Home and Start Arrangements	Begin the process based on any pre-arranged plans or wishes.
Contact the Deceased's Employer	Inform them of the death and inquire about benefits or dues.
Begin Obituary Preparation	Draft and submit an obituary to appropriate media if desired.
Review the Will and/or Trust	Identify the executor and start discussing the next steps.
Notify Key Financial Institutions	Inform banks and credit agencies of the death to prevent fraud.
Postpone or Redirect Mail	Contact the postal service to manage the deceased's mail.
Access Safe Deposit Boxes	Retrieve wills, trusts, and other key documents as needed.
Document and Begin Securing Assets	Start a list of assets for estate processing.
Locate Essential Documents	Find and organize important documents (will, trust, policies).
Consult with Legal and Financial Advisors	Seek professional advice for the next steps.
Plan for Immediate Financial Needs	Assess and arrange for urgent financial needs and bills.

This checklist is designed to help manage the initial tasks following a loved one's death. It's important to approach each step with care and consideration for all affected by the loss. Executors should prioritize tasks that prevent any financial harm or property loss and that respect the deceased's final wishes.

4.2 Choosing the Right Person

Stepping into the shoes of an executor or successor trustee is a significant responsibility, one that's pivotal in carrying out the final wishes of someone who's passed away. This chapter is a must-read for both the person creating the will (the grantor) and the nominated executor or successor trustee. It's crucial for the successor trustee to understand fully what this role entails. If you've been nominated, carefully consider the responsibilities and qualifications required. Accepting this role should come from a place of confidence and readiness. However, if after delving into this chapter, you feel the role isn't right for you, it's better to step aside early, allowing the grantor to find a more suitable candidate. Your careful consideration, whether you accept or decline, reflects your respect for the grantor's wishes and the gravity of the task at hand.

In this crucial section, we'll explore key considerations for choosing a successor trustee. Let's dive into:

1. **Age and Qualifications**: Understanding if the designated individual possesses the maturity and legal qualifications for the executor role.

2. **Residence**: Understanding how the executor's location can influence the estate management process.

3. **Relationship:** Recognizing the impact of the relationship between the executor/successor and the deceased and the beneficiaries on the execution of the will.

4. **Skills and Expertise**: Assessing the necessary skills and expertise required for managing the complexities of estate settlement.

It's essential for both the grantor and the prospective successor trustee to carefully evaluate these considerations. The ideal candidate should not only align with the deceased's final wishes but also possess the capability and willingness to undertake the significant responsibilities that come with managing an estate. It's a decision that warrants thoughtful deliberation, as the chosen individual will play a key role in honoring and executing the final intentions of the departed.

COMMON MISTAKE ALERT: Choosing a successor trustee based on birth order

One common error in estate planning is selecting an executor or successor trustee based on birth order, often the firstborn child. While this might seem like a natural choice, birth order alone is not an indicator of suitability for such a responsible role. It's crucial to look beyond familial hierarchy and consider other key factors, such as responsibility, financial acumen, and impartiality. The ideal candidate should possess the right mix of skills and temperament to manage your estate effectively, irrespective of their position in the family. Remember, the goal is to ensure a smooth and fair handling of your legacy.

COMMON MISTAKE ALERT: Assigning co-executors without clear roles

Appointing multiple executors or trustees with equal authority sounds inclusive, but beware - it can backfire. While collaboration can work wonders, in estate matters, it often breeds confusion and delay. Think of it as having two quarterbacks trying to run the same play – chaos ensues. Plus, there's a risk of the "someone else will handle it" mindset, where crucial tasks fall through the cracks. If you do choose co-representatives, clearly define their roles to avoid gridlocks, or better yet, supplement a family member with an impartial professional to steer the ship smoothly.

1. **Age and Qualifications:** Choosing the right executor is a bit like selecting a relay team captain – you want someone who's likely to be around for the long haul. Ideally, they should be younger than you, but not so young that they lack the necessary maturity or experience. Minors are definitely out of the running. It's like asking a high school athlete to coach a professional team – not a great fit. While it might feel odd to bypass your peers for a younger candidate, remember it's about ensuring the smooth handling of your estate. And hey, a backup plan is always a smart move, just like having a reserve player ready to jump in. So, if you're considering someone your age, also think about a 'plan B' – a successor executor, to cover all bases.

2. **Residence:** When pondering the role of executor or successor trustee, remember it's not just about legal or financial savvy. It's also about being there, both literally and figuratively. If you're often jet-setting for work or living states away, think twice. Settling an estate isn't a remote job; it often demands your physical presence, and your travel costs could nibble away at the estate's funds. Some states are picky too, preferring or even insisting on local executors. They might let out-of-towners take the helm, but with strings attached, like appointing a local go-to for legal stuff. It's about being in the trenches when it counts, not just on paper.

3. **Relationship:** When it comes to crafting a will or trust, it's pretty common for people to think about naming someone close to them—like a spouse, sibling, or adult child—as the executor or successor trustee. Now, there's no rule saying a family member or someone who's getting a piece of the pie can't be serve this function. In fact, having a family member in this role can save some money since they sometimes don't charge fees. However, it's a bit like walking a tightrope. Family dynamics can be tricky, and even if

they're usually smooth, adding money and various desires to the mix can stir up a hornet's nest of emotions and disagreements. So, if you're considering a family member for this job, you've got to think hard about whether they can handle the pressure and keep things fair and square. Just remember, being an executor or successor trustee isn't just about being related; it's about being able to handle the job with a cool head and a fair hand.

4. **Skills and Expertise**: When weighing the decision to take on the role of executor or successor trustee, particularly for estates encompassing complex elements like diverse real estate, ongoing litigation, or intricate investment portfolios, assess your own skill set realistically. If you feel the estate's complexity is beyond your expertise, suggesting a bank or trust company as executor or trustee is a valid alternative, though their fees can be substantial for larger estates. Remember, as an executor or successor trustee, you're empowered to seek professional assistance for legal, accounting, and financial management, the costs of which the estate will cover. The key qualities for success in these roles are common sense, integrity, diligence, and a steadfast approach.

Your Right to Decline

It's crucial to remember that as an executor or successor trustee, you're not just bound at the start; you have the option to step down at any point, even after formal court appointment and initiating estate administration. While such a decision might interrupt the estate's orderly settlement, it's essential to know that this option exists. Life is unpredictable, and unforeseen circumstances in your life might necessitate this choice. It's a safety valve worth keeping in mind.

Should you take the job?

Usually, a testator will consult with their chosen executor or successor trustee, often when a will or trust is being drafted or updated, to confirm their willingness to serve. While you can always decline initially or later, including after the testator's passing or even after formal appointment by the court, it's essential to weigh the decision carefully. Age, health concerns, potential conflicts with beneficiaries, or simply not wanting the responsibility are all valid reasons to consider declining.

However, concerns about managing a complex estate can often be mitigated by hiring professionals like estate lawyers, appraisers, and financial consultants, whose fees can be paid from estate funds. If you possess organizational skills, prudence, and attention to detail, these qualities can make the role manageable. Furthermore, being involved in organizing the testator's assets before their passing can simplify or even bypass the probate process, easing the burden after their death. Serving as an executor or successor trustee, especially for a friend or relative, can be a deeply meaningful gesture of respect and closure.

COMMON MISTAKE ALERT: Failing to reassess your executor or successor trustee

It's essential for a testator to periodically review and possibly update their choice of executor or successor trustee. Life changes, such as relocation, health issues, or shifts in availability, can impact an individual's ability to fulfill these roles effectively. Similarly, new, better-suited candidates may emerge over time. For instance, in my own experience, my father initially appointed my elder brother as the successor trustee. However, as I gained more industry experience, he updated his choice, recognizing that my skill set was more aligned with the responsibilities. It's crucial not to hesitate in making such changes, when necessary, as they can significantly influence the smooth execution of your estate plan.

4.2 (a) Questions FOR Your Executor/Successor Trustee

Here are the questions rephrased for assessing a potential executor or successor trustee, with potential red flags and their implications, as well as additional insightful questions. By asking these questions, you aim to gauge not only the willingness but also the suitability of the individual for the critical role of executor or successor trustee. The responses can reveal a lot about their capabilities and mindset, which are essential for ensuring that the estate is managed according to the deceased's wishes.

1.   Have you had experience serving as an executor or handling estate matters before?

- **Red Flag**: "No, but it seems straightforward enough."
- This may indicate a lack of appreciation for the complexity of the role.
- **Additional Question**: "Can you provide examples of how you've dealt with complex issues in the past?"

2. Are you able to dedicate the necessary time and effort to manage the estate effectively?

- **Red Flag**: "I'm usually swamped, but I guess I can try to fit it in somewhere."
- Implies a lack of commitment and priority for the significant responsibilities involved.
- **Additional Question**: "How do you plan to balance these new responsibilities with your current ones?"

3. Can you describe your organizational skills and how they would apply to executing an estate?

- **Red Flag**: "I'm not really an organized person; I tend to go with the flow."
- Suggests a possible inability to manage the detailed and structured tasks required.
- **Additional Question**: "What systems do you use to keep track of important tasks and deadlines?"

4. How comfortable are you with mediating disputes among beneficiaries, should they arise?

- **Red Flag**: "I avoid conflict whenever possible and prefer not to get involved."
- Indicates a reluctance to address potentially critical aspects of estate administration.
- **Additional Question**: "How would you approach a situation where beneficiaries disagree?"

5. Do you understand financial matters well, including accounting and record-keeping?

- **Red Flag**: "Finance isn't my strong suit, but I can always learn on the job."
- Suggests a risk for financial mismanagement or errors.
- **Additional Question**: "Have you ever managed large budgets or financial portfolios?"

6. Can you assure me of your integrity and trustworthiness in managing the estate?

- **Red Flag**: "I guess so, though everyone bends the rules now and then."
- Raises serious concerns about ethical standards and adherence to fiduciary duties.
- **Additional Question**: "Can you provide an example of a time when your integrity was tested?"

7. Given the unpredictability of life, do you think you will be able to serve as executor for the duration needed?

- **Red Flag**: "Hard to say, my own health and plans are quite uncertain."
- Uncertainty here can compromise the completion of long-term estate proceedings.
- **Additional Question**: "What are your long-term commitments that might affect your ability to serve?"

8. Do you feel comfortable with the responsibilities of being an executor and managing my estate?

- **Red Flag**: "Honestly, it's a bit outside my comfort zone, but I don't want to let you down."
- Reluctance or discomfort could lead to ineffective estate management.
- **Additional Question**: "What motivates you to take on the role of executor or successor trustee?"

4.2 (b) Questions FROM your Executor/Successor Trustee

Here are the reformulated questions to ask when being requested to serve as an executor or successor trustee, with potential red flags for each and additional insightful questions. When considering taking on the role of an executor or successor trustee, it's important to understand the expectations, the level of involvement, and whether the estate has been properly structured with professional advice. These questions will help you gauge the scope of the role and whether you can commit to the responsibilities with the seriousness and dedication they require.

1. Can you provide an overview of your estate plan and its goals?

- **Red Flag**: Vagueness or avoidance of specifics.
- **Insightful Question**: "How does your estate plan reflect your values and priorities?"

2. What specific responsibilities would I have as your executor?

- **Red Flag**: Lack of clear expectations.
- **Insightful Question**: "Can we outline a detailed list of duties and timelines?"

3. Is your will or trust prepared and am I named within it?

- **Red Flag**: No legal documentation in place.
- **Insightful Question**: "How often do you review and update your legal documents?"

4. Have you consulted an attorney about your estate plan?

- **Red Flag**: No professional legal advice sought.
- **Insightful Question**: "Can I have the attorney's contact for further clarity?"

5. Who are the beneficiaries and what are your intentions for each?

- **Red Flag**: Potential for conflict not addressed.
- **Insightful Question**: "Have you discussed your estate plan with the beneficiaries?"

6. Can you provide a list of assets, debts, and liabilities?

- **Red Flag**: Incomplete financial overview.
- **Insightful Question**: "Do we have up-to-date valuations for all significant assets?"

7. Are there other executors or professionals involved in your estate?

- **Red Flag**: Too many cooks in the kitchen without defined roles.
- **Insightful Question**: "How do you envision the collaboration between all parties?"

8. What are your expectations regarding compensation for this role?

- **Red Flag**: Unwillingness to discuss compensation.
- **Insightful Question**: "How do you see my role being valued, both in terms of responsibility and compensation?"

4.3 Ongoing Learning in the Realm of Estate Planning

Estate planning is a dynamic field, constantly evolving with changes in law, tax regulations, financial theories, technology advancements, and societal norms. For both the testator and the successor trustee or executor, staying informed is critical.

Ways to stay updated include:

- **Regular Consultations with Professionals**: Schedule periodic meetings with estate lawyers, financial advisors, and tax professionals.

- **Educational Workshops and Seminars**: Attend local or online seminars focused on estate planning trends and changes.

- **Subscriptions to Relevant Publications**: Subscribe to newsletters and journals that cover estate planning, tax laws, and financial management.

- **Online Courses and Webinars**: Utilize online platforms offering courses in estate planning and related fields.

- **Networking with Peers**: Join estate planning groups or forums to exchange knowledge and experiences.

- **Staying Informed on Legislative Changes**: Keep an eye on state and federal legislative developments that could impact estate planning.

- **Technology Adaptation**: Embrace new tools and software designed to streamline estate management and planning processes.

Committing time to learning and adapting is not just recommended; it's a necessity for anyone involved in estate planning. This ongoing education ensures that both the testator and the executor or successor trustee are equipped to handle the complexities of estate management effectively.
Here are a few examples of how a lack of ongoing learning could impact your plan.

1. **"Ignoring Legal Updates"**: Not keeping abreast of new estate laws can lead to significant legal missteps. For instance, failing to update a trust based on recent tax law changes could inadvertently increase tax liabilities or penalties for an estate, potentially leading to personal liability for the trustee.

2.   **"Overlooking Tax Changes"**: Tax regulations can shift dramatically, impacting estate planning strategies. An executor who isn't up-to-date with these changes might miss critical tax-saving opportunities or, worse, incur additional taxes and penalties for the estate.

3.   **"Neglecting Technological Advancements"**: In today's digital age, assets include digital properties like cryptocurrencies or online accounts. Not being aware of how to manage these digital assets can result in their loss or mismanagement, impacting the estate's overall value.

4.   **"Ignoring Societal Shifts"**: Social changes, such as new definitions of family units or inheritance rights, can significantly impact estate planning. Failing to adapt to these shifts might lead to disputes among beneficiaries or unintended exclusion of rightful heirs.

4.4 Trustee Fees and Expenses

As a trustee, you're entitled to compensation for your services in managing and settling the trust. Your fee should reflect your qualifications, the nature and complexity of your duties, and the trust's asset value. If multiple trustees are involved, the fee should be divided based on each trustee's responsibilities. In some states, trustee fees are regulated by statutes. However, if you're also a trust beneficiary, it might be more tax-efficient to forgo the fee, as trustee fees are taxable income, whereas inheritance from the trust isn't.

COMMON MISTAKE ALERT: Not taking a fee

While there are situations where not taking a fee makes sense, remember that managing a trust is work that warrants fair compensation. Don't feel obligated to work for free, even for family matters. Proper compensation reflects the importance and effort of the role. Stepping into the role of a successor trustee or executor is akin to being a coach who's also a key player in a long, demanding season. It's not just about strategizing; it's about being on the field, deeply involved in every play. This responsibility can consume a significant amount of your time and mental energy, time that you might otherwise spend on your career, family, or personal hobbies. Like a dedicated coach who sacrifices personal time for the team's success, you'll find this role taking up substantial space in your life. It's essential to weigh this commitment against your other responsibilities and passions.

4.5 Liabilities, Loyalties, Prudance and Protection

Liability of the Executor & Successor Trustee

Taking on the executor role places you in a position of trust, demanding diligent management of the estate's assets, settling debts accurately, and strictly following the will's instructions. Failing in these duties exposes you to legal risks. Poor estate management that leads to financial losses can prompt lawsuits from beneficiaries or creditors. Moreover, the court might strip you of your compensation or remove you for estate mismanagement. Protecting the estate with a surety bond, paid from estate funds, shields against inadvertent errors or misconduct. Documenting every action and maintaining open communication, as detailed in Section 7.4 "Communication & Documentation," is crucial for transparency and protection. This approach minimizes the risk of disputes or misunderstandings that could result in liability.

COMMON MISTAKE ALERT: Underestimating the importance of communication and documentation.

Neglecting thorough documentation and clear communication can lead to misunderstandings or disputes, potentially increasing your liability as an executor. Always keep detailed records and communicate proactively with all involved parties.

Maintaining Integrity & Loyalty

As an executor, you hold a fiduciary duty to the estate, its beneficiaries, and creditors. Your role demands unwavering loyalty to their interests, not personal gain. Direct purchasing of estate assets or using them for personal investments is generally off-limits unless explicitly allowed by the will or approved by the court. Even indirect purchases, if traced back to you, can be nullified unless passing through an impartial buyer at a fair price. Selling estate assets to relatives is permissible in some cases, but only if the transaction is fair and conducted in good faith. This is crucial to uphold the integrity of the executor's role and maintain the trust of all parties involved.

Diligence

As an executor, your responsibility is to manage the estate with the same care and skill as a reasonably diligent person would in their own affairs. This means you're not expected to generate profits or prevent every loss, but you must avoid recklessly diminishing the estate's assets. Should you become aware of risks in an investment, it's your duty to act wisely to protect the estate. For safety, you might choose federally insured options over riskier, high-yield investments. And if the will mandates immediate sale of securities, it's prudent to follow those directions without trying to predict market fluctuations.

COMMON MISTAKE ALERT: Neglecting professional advice

One critical misstep in estate management is not seeking professional advice when needed. It's important to recognize your own limits in knowledge and expertise. Estate situations, especially complex ones, often require specialized legal and financial insight. As an executor, you're tasked with finding the right solutions, not just relying on personal assumptions or guesses. Therefore, consulting with financial advisors and legal professionals is not just advisable, it's a crucial part of responsibly managing the estate and ensuring all decisions are well-informed and legally sound. Avoid the pitfall of thinking you have all the answers and, instead, leverage the expertise available to you.

Chapter 5

Near Death – Embracing Transition

5.1 The Duality of Loss: Emotional and Administrative

5.2 The Importance of Healthcare Directives and Family Communication

    (a) Incapacity Planning

    (b) Disability and Long-Term Care

    (c) Power of Attorney and Healthcare Representatives

    (d) Final Arrangements and End-of-Life Care

5.3 Coping Strategies for the Emotional Burden

5.4 Resources for Guiding Through the Transition

Chapter 5 of our estate planning journey, "Near Death - Embracing Transition," is a sensitive yet crucial exploration of the emotional and administrative challenges families face during the final stages of a loved one's life. It's a more succinct chapter, reflective of a journey into a realm where emotions intertwine with practicalities, a path less traveled in the financial narrative.

This chapter serves as a heartfelt acknowledgment of the duality that accompanies the end-of-life transition. It's about navigating the complex emotional landscape while managing the necessary administrative tasks. Think of it as a coach offering guidance to a team during the most critical part of the game, where strategy must be balanced with empathy.

Here, we delve into the importance of clear and compassionate communication, akin to a team huddle in crucial game moments. It's important to ensure that everyone is on the same page, understanding both the emotional and practical aspects of the transition.

A significant portion of the chapter is dedicated to coping strategies, similar to a coach's playbook for handling challenging phases. It provides practical advice and emotional support techniques to help families manage the weight of loss.

The chapter also serves as a gentle guide to available resources, offering directions to help navigate this challenging time. It acknowledges that while it provides a starting point, there are many specialized resources that offer deeper insights into these aspects.

Interwoven throughout the chapter are Common Mistake Alerts (CMAs), drawing from personal experiences and lessons learned within my own family, as elaborated in Chapter 8. These CMAs serve as cautionary tales and advice, helping you to anticipate and avoid potential pitfalls in this emotionally charged journey.

Remember, this chapter, while brief, is an integral part of our estate planning guide. It's a testament to the importance of addressing the emotional alongside the administrative, ensuring a holistic approach to one of life's most profound transitions.

5.1 The Duality of Loss: Emotional and Administrative

In the game of life, especially as it nears its closing chapters, we often find ourselves at the intersection of profound emotions and critical logistics. This period can be likened to the tense final moments of a crucial game, where every decision, every action, takes on heightened significance. Just as a seasoned coach in a high-stakes match must balance strategy with empathy, those navigating end-of-life situations must find equilibrium between managing grief and tackling essential tasks.

COMMON MISTAKE ALERT: Overlooking emotional support

It's a common oversight during these times to become engrossed in the administrative and logistical aspects of estate and legacy planning. Tasks like sorting out legal documents, managing financial affairs, and coordinating with various entities often take center stage. However, focusing solely on these tasks can inadvertently lead to emotional neglect. This is where we need to remember that, much like a cohesive team, emotional support is crucial for resilience and strength.

In the midst of organizing and executing plans, it's vital to pause and acknowledge the emotional landscape of those involved. Grieving is a deeply personal and complex process, one that doesn't adhere to a set timeline or a one-size-fits-all approach. People experience and express grief in diverse ways, and recognizing this diversity is essential. Just as a good coach understands the individual personalities and needs of their team members, we too must strive to understand and support the unique emotional journeys of our family members.

Moreover, emotional support shouldn't be viewed as a separate task from the logistical aspects of estate planning. Instead, it should be woven seamlessly into every interaction and decision. This could mean taking the time to have meaningful conversations, listening to concerns, sharing memories, or simply being present in a supportive way. It's about creating a space where emotions are acknowledged and respected, where family members feel heard and supported.

This balance isn't easy to strike. It requires patience, empathy, and often, the courage to face our own emotions. It also involves recognizing when professional help, such as grief counseling, might be beneficial. Remember, a team's strength is not just in its strategies and plans, but also in its unity and emotional resilience.

As we delve deeper into the nuances of estate and legacy planning, let's carry with us the understanding that while the logistical aspects are undeniably important, the emotional well-being of those involved is equally, if not more, crucial. It's this dual focus that can truly honor the legacy of a loved one, ensuring that their final chapter is managed with both efficiency and compassion.

Physical Symptoms	Emotional Symptoms	Behavioral Symptoms
Sleep disturbances	Sadness	Forgetfulness
Shortness of breath	Anger	Worrying more about others
Tightness in throat	Guilt	Prolonged withdrawal from normal activity.
Physical distress	Anxiety	
Weight change	Loneliness	

5.2 The Importance of Health Care Directives and Family Communication

Clear Healthcare Directives: Just as a coach outlines a game plan for the team, your healthcare directives need to be explicitly stated. This clarity ensures your wishes are respected and followed, preventing the kind of misunderstandings that can lead to familial discord.

WHAT HAPPENS WHEN YOU DON'T HAVE A/AN...	
Advanced Directive	**Living Will**
Undesired treatments	Unwanted life-sustaining treatments may be applied
Disagreements on treatments among family members	Treatments may conflict with personal, cultural, or religious beliefs
Legal disputes causing treatment delays	Delayed decisions may lead to prolonged suffering and expense
Emotional stress	Emotional burdens from making critical decisions

COMMON MISTAKE ALERT: Miscommunication about healthcare wishes

Miscommunication about healthcare wishes is akin to a team misinterpreting the game plan. To prevent this, discussions about your healthcare preferences must be clear and thorough, much like a well-called play in a crucial game.

5.2 (a) Incapacity Planning

Incapacity planning is the strategic preparation for potential physical or mental inability to manage one's affairs. It's an essential component of a comprehensive estate plan, safeguarding against the unexpected twists in life's journey, much like a team's contingency planning for unforeseen events during a game.

Tips for Incapacity Planning:

- **Choose Wisely**: Select individuals who are trustworthy and capable of making decisions that align with your values and wishes. Consider their ability to handle complex financial matters and medical decisions.

- **Legal Documents**: Utilize powers of attorney and living wills to legally document your preferences. Ensure they are regularly updated to reflect any changes in your life circumstances or wishes.

- **Communicate Your Wishes**: Have in-depth discussions with the people you appoint to ensure they understand your desires and are willing to act on your behalf when needed.

- **Regular Reviews**: Like a team revisits its strategies, regularly review your incapacity plan to ensure it remains relevant and effective.

5.2 (b) Disability and Long-Term Care

Considering disability and long-term care is an acknowledgment of life's unpredictability. The cost of long-term care can be astronomical, much like unexpected expenses can hit a sports team's budget.

Tips for Disability and Long-Term Care Planning

- **Insurance**: Investigate different types of disability and long-term care insurance. Understand the coverage, limitations, and costs associated with each policy.

- **Savings**: Consider setting aside funds specifically for long-term care needs. This financial cushion can provide peace of mind and security.

- **Government Programs**: Research government assistance programs like Medicaid, which may offer support for long-term care under certain conditions.

Estate Impact: Understand how long-term care costs could impact your estate and the inheritance you wish to leave behind.

5.2 (c) Power of Attorney and Healthcare Representatives

Appointing a Power of Attorney (POA) and healthcare representatives is like having backups ready on the sidelines, ensuring the game continues smoothly even if the key player is sidelined.

Types of Power of Attorney	USE	MOST USEFUL FOR
Durable Power of Attorney	Can be used whether the Principal is incapacitated or not.	Estate planning and delegating your financial affairs.
Springing Power of Attorney	Activates on a future date or when a specified event occurs.	Planning for your incapacity or absence.
Special Power of Attorney	Allows an Agent to perform only one or two specific duties.	Delegating tasks to experts (such as realtors or brokers)
Medical Power of Attorney	Lets the Agent make medical decision for the Principal.	Planning for medical emergencies in the future.

Tips for Selecting POA and Healthcare Representatives:

- **Responsibility Matching**: Ensure that the representatives' skills match the responsibilities they may need to undertake.

- **Legal Authority**: Work with an attorney to grant the correct legal authority to your representatives, including limitations to prevent overreach.

- **Alternates**: Have alternates in place in case your primary choice is unavailable when needed.

- **Clarity of Role**: Make sure your representatives understand the extent and limits of their roles to prevent abuse of power.

5.2 (d) Final Arrangements and End-of-Life Care

Planning for end-of-life care and final arrangements is a profound act of consideration for those you love, akin to a coach's end-of-game strategy that ensures a dignified exit.

Item	Location / Name	ID Numbers
Personal Information:		
Full legal name		
Date of birth		
Social Security number		
Contact information for primary care physician		
Contact information for specialists		
Health care proxy and durable power of attorney		
Durable power of attorney for finances		
Emergency contact list of family and close friends		
Information for counselor, or emotional support		
Medical Details:		
List of current medications and dosages		
List of known allergies		
Medical insurance details, including policy numbers		
Specific medical wishes, including DNR if applicable		
Financial Information:		
Overview of basic financial records		
List of monthly bills and obligations		
Legal Documents:		
Copies of wills and trusts		
Any advance directives or living wills		
Housing and Care:		
Information about current living arrangements		
Contact details for landlords or property managers		
Insurance Policies:		
Details of life insurance policies		
Long-term care insurance details, if any		
Living Arrangement Details:		
Keys to home or security codes		
Pet care instructions		
Maintenance Medications:		
Prescription refill schedules		
Pharmacy contact information		
Assistive Device Information:		
Details and instructions for hearing aids, pacemakers, mobility aids, etc.		
Personal Preferences:		
Dietary restrictions or preferences		
Daily routine or caregiving instructions		
Access to Communication Devices:		
Cell phone and charger		
Emergency button or medical alert system details		

This checklist is a general guide. Executors should always consider seeking professional legal and financial advice to navigate the nuances of estate administration.

Tips for Final Arrangements:

- **Document Your Wishes**: Clearly outline your preferences for funeral, memorial services, and burial or cremation. Include as many details as you wish to be followed.

- **Financial Planning**: Set aside funds or consider prepaying for certain services to alleviate the financial burden on your loved ones.

- **Legal Directives**: Advance directives and living wills can specify your wishes for medical treatment at the end of life.

- **Open Discussions**: Have heartfelt conversations with your family about your wishes to prepare them emotionally and logistically for when the time comes.

By giving thorough consideration to these aspects, you're not just preparing for eventualities but also providing clear guidance and peace of mind for your loved ones, ensuring your wishes are respected and accomplished with the dignity and respect they deserve.

5.3 Coping Strategies for the Emotional Burden

In the aftermath of loss, every individual's journey through grief is unique, mirroring the diverse ways athletes handle the pressures of their sport. Here are some effective coping strategies, each suited to different needs and personalities:

1. **Group Counseling**: Ideal for those who find comfort in shared experiences. Like a team debrief after a tough match, group counseling provides a supportive environment where individuals can connect with others facing similar challenges, offering mutual understanding and collective healing.

2. **Personal Therapy**: Best suited for individuals who prefer a more private approach to processing emotions, akin to a one-on-one coaching session. Personal therapy offers a safe space to explore feelings deeply, guided by a professional who can tailor the approach to individual needs.

3. **Sharing Stories and Memories**: For those who find solace in reminiscing sharing stories and memories can be a therapeutic way to honor the

deceased. Much like a team reminiscing about past victories, this approach helps keep the loved one's memory alive and can bring comfort and a sense of continuity.

4.   **Engaging in Creative Outlets**: Creative expression, whether through art, writing, music, or gardening, can be a powerful tool for processing grief. This strategy works well for individuals who find healing in expressing themselves creatively, like an athlete channeling emotion into their sport.

5.   **Physical Activity**: Physical exercise, such as walking, yoga, or sports, can be beneficial for those who cope better with physical expression. It's akin to an athlete using physical exertion as a way to manage stress and emotions.

6.   **Spiritual Practices**: For those who find strength in their faith or spirituality, engaging in religious or spiritual practices can offer comfort and perspective. This can be similar to athletes who draw motivation and resilience from their beliefs.

Each of these strategies provides a way to navigate the emotional turmoil of loss, but it's crucial to choose the one that resonates most with you. Just as athletes select techniques that best suit their style and strengths, individuals should opt for coping mechanisms that align with their personality and comfort level. Remember, acknowledging and processing grief is as vital to emotional health as physical training is to an athlete's performance. Ignoring personal grief can lead to prolonged emotional distress, impacting overall well-being and the ability to move forward.

COMMON MISTAKE ALERT: Ignoring personal grief

Not addressing your own grief can lead to emotional strain. It's essential to process your emotions, just as a player needs to address their mental state for optimal performance.

5.4 Resources for Guiding Through the Transition

As you navigate the challenging transition after a loved one's passing, think of it as a team drawing on its full range of resources to aid recovery and resilience. Embracing available support services can significantly ease the journey, providing comfort and guidance much like a coach and medical team assist an athlete through challenging times. Here's how you can effectively use these resources:

1.   **Hospice Care & Palliative Care**: Hospice and palliative care, often used interchangeably, are similar yet distinct forms of support, each playing a unique role much like different positions on a sports team. Here's how they compare and contrast:

- **Hospice Care**: Hospice care is like the specialized coach who steps in during the final phase of the game – it's designed for the end-of-life stage when curative treatment is no longer pursued. The focus is on comfort and quality of life, providing comprehensive care that addresses physical, emotional, and spiritual needs. Hospice care supports not just the individual but also their family, offering guidance and emotional support during this challenging time.

- **Palliative Care**: Palliative care can be likened to a versatile player who assists throughout the entire game, regardless of the stage or score. It's appropriate at any stage of a serious illness, whether terminal or chronic, and can be provided alongside curative treatments. The goal is to relieve symptoms, pain, and stress, thereby improving the quality of life for both the patient and their family. Palliative care is a multidisciplinary approach that addresses the broader needs of the patient, including physical, emotional, and spiritual well-being.

- **Similarity**: Both hospice and palliative care prioritize comfort and quality of life, focusing on relieving pain and other distressing symptoms. They offer a holistic approach that includes emotional and spiritual support, akin to a team providing comprehensive care for an athlete.

- **Difference**: The key difference lies in the timing and purpose. Palliative care can begin at diagnosis and continue alongside curative treatments. In contrast, hospice care begins after treatment of the illness is stopped and when it is clear that the person is not going to survive the illness.

Incorporating hospice and palliative care into an estate plan or end-of-life decision-making is crucial. It ensures that the individual's preferences for comfort and care are respected, much like a coach respects an athlete's choices for their training and recovery. It's about making informed decisions that align with the individual's wishes and providing the best possible quality of life in their final journey.

2.   **Counseling Services**: Grief counselors or therapists are like personal trainers for emotional health. They offer expert guidance and support to navigate the complex emotions of grief, helping individuals process their feelings and find ways to cope.

3.   **Support Groups**: Joining a support group can be as beneficial as a team debrief after a crucial game. It's a space to share experiences and feelings with others who understand what you're going through, offering mutual support and understanding.

4.   **Legal and Financial Advisors**: Engaging with professionals like estate lawyers and financial advisors can provide clarity and assistance in managing the practical aspects of a loved one's estate. Think of them as the strategists and analysts in your team, helping you navigate the legal and financial complexities.

5.   **Community and Religious Organizations**: For many, support from community or religious organizations plays a vital role, offering a sense of belonging and a network of care. These groups can be a source of comfort and practical assistance, similar to a supportive fanbase or community around a sports team.

6.   **Online Resources and Literature**: There's a wealth of information available online, including websites, forums, and books on grief and estate management. These resources are like the extensive playbook and training manuals available to athletes, providing knowledge and strategies to tackle the challenges ahead.

COMMON MISTAKE ALERT: Neglecting available resources

Neglecting available resources can be like a sports team ignoring their support staff's expertise and training tools. It's essential to leverage these resources for guidance, support, and ease of mind during this difficult transition. They're there to help you manage the complexities and emotions of this period, ensuring you don't have to face these challenges alone.

Chapter 6

Shortly After Death – Charting Through Turmoil

6.1 Immediate Actions and Precautions Post-loss

6.2 Emotional Dimensions of Estate Administration

6.3 Strategies for Managing Grief and Family Dynamics

6.4 Self-care and Building Resilience

Chapter 6, titled "Shortly After Death - Charting Through Turmoil," approaches the sensitive period following a loved one's passing with a blend of practical guidance and emotional insight. This chapter is akin to navigating through a storm, focusing on balancing immediate responsibilities with the emotional weight of loss.

In this chapter, we explore the immediate steps that need to be taken after a loved one's passing. It involves taking control of the situation, much like a captain steadying a ship during a storm, ensuring that critical tasks are handled amidst the emotional upheaval.

The emotional aspects of estate administration are given due attention, recognizing that managing an estate is not just a series of tasks but a journey through complex family dynamics and personal grief. This section is like a guide through a maze of emotions, providing strategies to handle grief and maintain family harmony during this tumultuous time.

Self-care and resilience are emphasized as crucial elements. Just as a weary traveler must find strength to continue, those dealing with estate administration need to take care of their well-being to manage the responsibilities effectively.

Chapter 6 doesn't shy away from the softer skills needed during this challenging period. It acknowledges the dual nature of the executor's role – as an administrator and a compassionate family member – and offers a compassionate, holistic approach to navigating the aftermath of a loss. This chapter aims to be a guiding light through one of life's most challenging phases, providing support and clarity when it's needed the most.

6.1 Immediate Actions and Precautions Post-loss

When dealing with the immediate aftermath of a loved one's passing, it's important to address both emotional and practical aspects:

Task	Details
Obtain Official Death Certificate	Request multiple copies for various administrative procedures.
Secure the Deceased's Property	Ensure the deceased's residence and personal property is secure.
Arrange Care for Dependents and Pets	Ensure children, elderly dependents, and pets have care.
Notify Close Family and Friends	Share the news in a respectful and considerate manner.
Select a Funeral Home and Start Arrangements	Begin the process based on any pre-arranged plans or wishes.
Contact the Deceased's Employer	Inform them of the death and inquire about benefits or dues.
Begin Obituary Preparation	Draft and submit an obituary to appropriate media if desired.
Review the Will and/or Trust	Identify the executor and start discussing the next steps.
Notify Key Financial Institutions	Inform banks and credit agencies of the death to prevent fraud.
Postpone or Redirect Mail	Contact the postal service to manage the deceased's mail.
Access Safe Deposit Boxes	Retrieve wills, trusts, and other key documents as needed.
Document and Begin Securing Assets	Start a list of assets for estate processing.
Locate Essential Documents	Find and organize important documents (will, trust, policies).
Consult with Legal and Financial Advisors	Seek professional advice for the next steps.
Plan for Immediate Financial Needs	Assess and arrange for urgent financial needs and bills.

This checklist is designed to help manage the initial tasks following a loved one's death. It's important to approach each step with care and consideration for all affected by the loss. Executors should prioritize tasks that prevent any financial harm or property loss and that respect the deceased's final wishes.

- **Emotional Health:** Acknowledge your grief and allow yourself to process it. You might experience various stages of loss. Prioritize self-care, as it's like putting on your oxygen mask first before assisting others.

- **Stay Calm and Trust the Plan:** Embrace a thoughtful pace, avoiding rushed decisions. This approach aligns with the wisdom of "Go slow to go fast." In your role, it's your responsibility to set the tone, reminding family members of the process's timeline and ensuring decisions are made when appropriate. Your calm demeanor can serve as a reassuring influence, fostering confidence among family members in your ability to manage the estate effectively.

- **Engage Your Support Team:** Reach out to your network of family, friends, and professional advisors. Their perspectives can provide comfort and guidance.

- **Prioritize Immediate Tasks:** Create a checklist of urgent tasks, such as arranging the funeral, securing the deceased's property, and notifying relevant institutions. Focus on these before moving on to more complex estate matters.

- **Follow the Plan**: Once you've addressed the immediate needs, proceed methodically with the executor duties, keeping the broader estate plan in mind. Remember, it's a process, not a race.

COMMON MISTAKE ALERT: Rushing decisions or neglecting self-care during the initial grieving phase

This can lead to mistakes and additional stress. It's vital to balance emotional well-being with the execution of duties. Remember, the entire timeline is detailed in Chapter 7 of this book.

6.2 Emotional Dimensions of Estate Administration

Estate planning, at its core, is not just a legal or financial process but an emotional journey. It involves confronting the inevitability of mortality and the legacy one wishes to leave behind. This journey can evoke a range of emotions:

Physical Symptoms	Emotional Symptoms	Behavioral Symptoms
Sleep disturbances	Sadness	Forgetfulness
Shortness of breath	Anger	Worrying more about others
Tightness in throat	Guilt	Prolonged withdrawal from normal activity.
Physical distress	Anxiety	
Weight change	Loneliness	

- **Reflection and Acceptance:** Accepting the reality of one's mortality and reflecting on life's achievements and values.

- **Family Dynamics:** Navigating complex family relationships and anticipating potential conflicts or misunderstandings.

- **Sense of Responsibility:** Feeling the weight of ensuring loved ones are cared for and wishes are honored.

- **Legacy Concerns:** Deciding how to be remembered and what values or memories to pass on.

- **Relief and Peace of Mind:** Experiencing comfort in knowing that affairs are in order, reducing the burden on loved ones.

Estate planning is deeply personal, intertwined with one's life story and relationships, making it an emotionally charged task. It's essential to approach it with sensitivity, considering not only the legal and financial aspects but also the emotional well-being of oneself and loved ones.

6.3 Strategies for Managing Grief and Family Dynamics

Managing family dynamics in estate planning is akin to navigating a complex team sport where each player has different motivations and goals. The key is to develop strategies that accommodate diverse perspectives and foster harmony.

- **Open Communication:** Encourage honest discussions about expectations and concerns. It's like a team huddle where everyone gets a chance to voice their thoughts.

- **Inclusivity**: Ensure all family members feel heard and valued, similar to recognizing each player's unique contribution to a team.

- **Flexibility**: Be prepared to adjust plans as family circumstances change, much like a coach adapts strategies mid-game.

- **Professional Guidance:** Involve experts like family counselors or mediators for unbiased perspectives, similar to bringing in a referee for fair play.

- **Education:** Educate family members about estate planning basics, akin to a team studying the rulebook together.

COMMON MISTAKE ALERT: Overlooking individual differences

Failing to acknowledge and respect individual differences within the family can lead to misunderstandings and conflicts. It's like a coach ignoring the diverse skills and needs of their team members, which can weaken the team's overall performance. Recognize and address these differences proactively to ensure a cohesive family plan.

Step	Task	Details
Preparation		
Set the Agenda	Define the topics to be discussed.	Include items such as estate overview, document locations, and roles.
Choose a Date and Time	Select a date that works for all key participants.	Consider family schedules and time zones for remote members.
Select a Location	Choose a comfortable and private space.	Ensure it's a neutral setting, or select an online platform if needed.
Anticipate Potential Conflicts	Identify possible areas of dispute and plan to address them.	Proactively discuss and resolve any known points of contention.
Prepare Documentation	Gather all relevant estate planning documents.	Include wills, trusts, POAs, and any other financial documents.
Conducting the Meeting		
Open the Meeting	Start with introductions and the purpose.	Acknowledge the importance of the meeting and everyone's presence.
Review the Agenda	Go over what will be discussed.	Ensure everyone understands the scope of the meeting.
Facilitate Discussion	Encourage open communication.	Allow each person to speak and encourage questions.
Consider Third Party Help	Identify areas where professionals could help.	Determine if legal, tax, accounting, insurance, or counseling expertise is required.
Manage Conflict Avoidance	Encourage factual discussion and appreciate all viewpoints.	Promote understanding and aim to prevent emotional escalation.
Address Estate Details	Explain the estate plan clearly.	Use simple language to discuss documents, decisions, and processes.
Discuss Roles and Expectations	Clarify the role of each person involved.	Define responsibilities of executors, trustees, and beneficiaries.
Provide Support Information	Offer resources for further help.	Share contact information for attorneys, advisors, etc.
Follow-Up		
Summarize Key Points	Recap the main topics covered.	Ensure everyone has a clear understanding of the discussion.
Document the Meeting	Keep a written record of what was discussed.	Record decisions made and any assigned action items.
Set Next Steps	Outline future tasks and meetings.	Include timelines for completing any necessary tasks.
Offer Availability	Be available for follow up questions.	Let family members know how they can reach you post-meeting.
Post-Meeting Actions		
Distribute Summary	Send out a writen meeting summary to all participants.	Provide a written recap and any relevant documents discussed.
Schedule Next Meeting	Plan for the next family meeting if needed.	Set a tentative date for future discussions or updates.
Follow Up on Tasks	Ensure action items are being addressed.	Check in with individuals responsible for tasks to offer assistance.

This checklist is for general guidance only and not a substitute for professional advice. Users should consult with appropriate professionals for specific advice tailored to their situation. The creator of this checklist is not responsible for any actions taken based on its content.

6.4 Self-care and Building Resilience

Self-care and building resilience during estate planning are essential, much like a player maintaining their fitness and mental strength throughout a season.

- **Prioritize Your Health**: Just as athletes need rest and recovery, give yourself breaks to recharge.

- **Seek Support**: Don't go it alone. Lean on friends, family, or professionals for support, akin to a player seeking a coach's guidance.

- **Maintain Perspective**: Remember the bigger picture and long-term goals, like a team focusing on the season's end.

- **Practice Mindfulness:** Stay present and grounded, similar to an athlete staying focused during a game.

Chapter 7

Wrapping Up a Life – Executor & Successor Trustee Duties

7.1 Timeline and Expectations

7.2 Professional Roles and Their Significance

7.3 The Importance of Organization

7.4 Communication and Documentation

7.5 Taxes

- **(a)** Federal Income Tax
- **(b)** Federal Estate Tax Exemptions
- **(c)** The Gift Tax
- **(d)** Generation-Skipping Transfer Tax
- **(e)** Valuation of the Gross Estate
- **(f)** Deductions
- **(g)** Paying the Federal Estate Tax
- **(h)** State and Local Income Tax
- **(i)** State Death Taxes
- **(j)** State Inheritance Taxes
- **(k)** State Estate Taxes

7.6 Distribution and Final Accounting

Chapter 7, titled "Wrapping Up a Life – Executor and Successor Trustee Duties," delves into the pragmatic and business-like aspects of finalizing an individual's life affairs. This chapter aligns more closely with the logical, structured approach of business thinking, a mindset that I personally resonate with. It underscores the importance of recognizing one's strengths and seeking help in areas of limitation, a key principle in effective estate management.

This chapter focuses on laying out a clear timeline and setting realistic expectations for the executor's journey. It's akin to charting a course, providing a roadmap for navigating the various stages of estate closure. This section is crucial for understanding the sequence of tasks and preparing for the responsibilities ahead.

The significance of professional roles in this process is highlighted. Just as a team relies on the unique skills of its members, the executor must understand how to effectively engage and collaborate with various professionals, from attorneys to financial advisors, each bringing their expertise to the table.

Organization is emphasized as a critical skill. Keeping track of documents, financial statements, and legal paperwork is akin to managing the backstage of a complex production, ensuring everything is in order for the final act.

Communication and documentation are identified as pivotal elements in the executor's role. These skills ensure clarity and prevent misunderstandings, similar to how a director communicates with a cast and crew to bring a vision to life.

A significant portion of the chapter is dedicated to navigating the complexities of taxes, a task requiring meticulous attention to detail and understanding of various tax laws and implications.

Finally, the chapter concludes with guidance on the distribution and final accounting, akin to the closing scene of a play, where all elements come together, and the executor's duties culminate in the successful closure of the estate.

Overall, Chapter 7 offers a comprehensive guide to the executor's duties, combining the precision and structure of business acumen with the sensitivity required in handling a departed loved one's affairs. It's a chapter about bringing closure with competence and care, ensuring the executor is well-equipped to handle the demands of this crucial role.

7.1 Timeline and Expectations

Taking on the role of an executor or successor trustee can feel like navigating through uncharted waters, especially when it comes to timing. Remember, the timeline I'm sharing is a rough estimate and might vary based on your specific location and situation. It's crucial to stay organized and mark your calendar with critical dates, setting reminders well in advance.

From my own experience, I understand the urge to complete tasks promptly. However, in the world of estate management, patience is key. You'll be working with various professionals who handle multiple clients, so it's essential to adjust to the pace of "business," which often seems slower than expected. This slower pace is not a sign of inefficiency but a reflection of the careful and thorough process needed in estate planning. Here's a general timeline to guide you through this journey:

Before Death:

- Identifying assets and securing real estate.
- Reviewing and understanding the will.
- Discussing special instructions with the testator for anatomical gifts, body disposal, and funeral rites.
- Meeting with family members, lawyers, and interested parties to understand the estate.

Shortly After Death:

- Identifying and collecting probate assets.
- Managing real estate, securities, or ongoing business.
- Notifying creditors and the post office.
- Filing claims for benefits like Social Security.
- Inspecting and securing properties, and evaluating insurance.
- Initiating ancillary probate for out-of-state properties.
- Opening an executor's bank account for estate funds.

Within 6 Months:

- Filing income, estate, or inheritance tax returns.
- Paying debts, taxes, and other expenses.
- Appraising assets for tax purposes.
- Publishing notice to creditors.
- Evaluating and making investment decisions.

Within 1 Year:

- Distributing remaining assets to beneficiaries.
- Preparing a final accounting and seeking court approval for fees.
- Seeking court approval for family allowance payments.
- Closing the estate, including resolving any legal disputes or will contests.

Keep in mind, this timeline is just a guide. Your situation might require different steps or a different pace. Stay flexible and consult with your professional team for advice tailored to your specific circumstances.

Time	Task	Details
Before Death		
	Locate & Confirm Estate Documents	Ensure documents are up-to-date and you have original executed versions.
	Understand Executor Duties	Research the legal duties and obligations.
	Understand Special Instructions	Anatomical gifts, body disposal, and funeral rites.
	Know the Key Contacts	Contact with key professionals, legal, tax, accounting, support, family and other.
	Gather Essential Information	Compile lists of assets, debts, account info, and key contacts.
Immediately After Death		
	Declaration of Death	Obtain and request multiple copies of the death certificate.
	Secure Property and Assets	Lock and secure all properties and assets.
	Notify Relevant Parties	Inform family, friends, and the estate attorney of the death.
	Seek Emotional Support	Reach out to counselors, clergy, or support groups.
Week One		
	Prepare Affair Documents	Organize and review necessary documents for estate planning.
	Initial Document Filing	File wills and legal documents based on attorney's advice.
	Estate Bank Account	Open a bank account for managing the estate's finances.
	Notify the Social Security Admiration and State Department of Health	Other agencies might need to be notified, check with your attorney
	Identify Trust Beneficiaries	Formal notification and waiting period could be required.
	Funeral Arrangements	Start funeral planning and coordination.
Week Two		
	Finalize Funeral Arrangements	Complete all funeral plans and payments.
	Inventory Assets	Document and appraise estate assets.
	Review Estate Finances	Assess immediate financial needs and obligations.
	Obtain Death Certificates	Ensure enough copies of the death certificate are available.
Week Three +		
	Continue Administration	Manage assets, pay bills, communicate with beneficiaries.
	Setup detailed Accounting system	Prepare and present detailed financial reports.
	Obtain trust EIN number	Seek legal and tax guidance.
	Tax Matters	File final tax returns and address estate taxes.
	Beneficiary Communication	Keep beneficiaries informed with clear, written updates.
	Notifications and Claims	Handle mail redirection, service cancellations, and file claims.
	Publishing Notice	Official publication could be required for creditors.
	Access Safety Deposit Box	Retrieve and inventory items in secure storage.
	Trust Account Transfers	Transfer assets into trust accounts as necessary into trustee name.
	Legal Challenges	Defend against any claims or actions against the estate.
	Debt Settlement	Pay off any outstanding debts.
	Asset Distribution	Distribute assets according post-probate and/or waiting period.
	Estate Closure	Complete formal estate closure after all tasks are completed.
Long-Term		
	Ongoing Communication	Regular updates to beneficiaries with good written records kept.
	Resolve Disputes	Mediate disputes and seek professional assistance if needed.
	Final or Ongoing Accounting	Provide detailed reports of all estate actions periodically.

This checklist is a general guide and the specific duties and timelines of an executor can vary based on the complexity of the estate, the laws of the state, and the particular wishes of the decedent. Executors should always consider seeking professional legal and financial advice to navigate the nuances of estate administration.

7.2 Professional Roles and Their Significance

In Section 2.3, we introduced your team of professionals essential for effective estate planning. As we delve deeper into their roles, it's important to understand the best ways to engage each one, maximizing their expertise while being mindful of your resources.

When engaging professionals for your estate planning, remember they should advise only within their area of expertise. Topics often overlap, so always verify with the primary expert. For instance, discuss tax ramifications with your real estate agent, but double-check with your tax professional. If you encounter conflicting advice, don't hesitate to seek a third opinion.

Regularly evaluate your professionals. If they no longer meet your needs or a better fit emerges, be ready to make changes. Remember, this is business, not personal. Your priority is the estate's well-being, so focus on what's best, not on loyalty or emotions. Stay agile and adaptive, like a coach making strategic plays for the team's success.

- **Attorney**: When working with an attorney, efficiency is key. They typically bill by the quarter-hour, so plan your consultations carefully. Organize your thoughts and questions, stay focused, and be clear to optimize your time and resources. Remember, legal advice isn't just about what's legally permissible; it's also about what's ethically sound and harmonious for your family dynamics. While a good attorney always prioritizes your interests, their advice should be balanced with consideration for family unity. Be mindful of legal disputes and who benefits from them – sometimes, it's better to avoid court to maintain peace and reduce costs.

- **Financial Advisor**: When engaging financial advisors, it's crucial to offer a complete view of your financial landscape. Share all relevant data and be upfront about your goals and requirements. Honesty is vital for effective financial planning. Encourage your advisors to present various strategies and perspectives. Don't hesitate to question and scrutinize their recommendations. Understand how they're compensated. If they're not directly paid by you, they might guide you towards in-house investments. These options may or may not align with your plan, so it's important to be vigilant and discerning in your choices.

- **Tax Professional**: Finding the right tax professional is akin to ensuring the perfect fit in a glove; it needs to align with your risk tolerance and personal convictions. Tax laws often leave room for interpretation, and tax advisors vary in their approach - some are more aggressive than others. It's crucial to gauge where they stand on this spectrum through questions and discussions. Remember, communication with your tax advisor is incredibly detailed, even more so than a confessional. Your organizational skills play a significant role here. Ultimately, the responsibility for the accuracy of your tax return lies with you, as you're the one signing it. So, it's essential to provide complete and timely information to avoid any potential missteps.

- **Real Estate Expert**: When addressing property matters, clear and specific communication is crucial. Prioritize preparing targeted questions and specific concerns about property management or investments for focused advice. Each property in your portfolio has a unique purpose, and understanding and effectively communicating these goals is essential. This approach ensures your real estate expert aligns their strategies with your objectives, leading to more effective management and investment decisions.

- **Family Counselor**: Openly discuss emotional aspects and family dynamics. They help navigate the personal side of estate planning, essential for maintaining family harmony. This is no time to be bashful, flush out any potentially difficult situations and find ways to help cope or mitigate a difficult situation.

- **Insurance Professional**: It's essential that your agent has a comprehensive understanding of your overall financial and personal situation. Regular communication is key. Make sure to touch base frequently, especially after significant life events that could impact your insurance needs. It's also a good practice to conduct an annual review of your policies. This ensures that your coverage continues to align with your evolving needs and helps you avoid overspending on unnecessary policies or missing out on essential coverage. Remember, in insurance, being well-informed can lead to significant savings

- **Business Advisor**: Involving a business advisor in the early stages of estate planning, especially when business interests are involved, is vital. It's important to provide them with detailed information about your business assets to receive tailored advice. Ensure that your advisor has expertise specific to your industry, as generic advice is often inadequate for complex business scenarios. If your estate includes multiple businesses, consider consulting several advisors, each specializing in different areas. This approach ensures comprehensive coverage of all business aspects, allowing for more effective and strategic estate planning. Remember, specialized knowledge can make a significant difference in handling intricate business affairs.

In all cases, remember that effective communication and preparedness are key. Each professional plays a specific role in your estate planning journey, and understanding how to best engage with them can streamline the process and ensure your estate is managed according to your wishes.

7.3 The Importance of Organization

Organization in estate planning is akin to having a well-oiled machine; it ensures everything runs smoothly and efficiently. Here are some ways to achieve and maintain this level of organization:

1. **Centralized Documentation**: Like a library with well-cataloged books, keep all your important documents in one place. This could be a physical file cabinet or digital cloud storage. Ensure documents like wills, trust agreements, insurance policies, real estate deeds, and investment records are easily accessible.

2. **Use of Technology**: In this digital age, leveraging technology is like having a supercomputer in your pocket. Use digital tools and apps for document storage, reminders, and tracking important dates. There are estate planning software and apps available that can help you keep track of documents, deadlines, and tasks. Remember, technology is there to make your life easier, so use it to its full potential.

3. **Regular Updates and Reviews**: Organizing isn't a one-time event; it's an ongoing process. Schedule regular times to review and update your documents. Life changes such as marriages, births, deaths, and significant financial changes should trigger a review. It's like tuning your instrument regularly to ensure it plays the right notes.

4. **Detailed Record-Keeping**: Keep detailed records of all transactions, communications, and decisions. This can include logs of phone calls, copies of emails, and notes from meetings. Think of it as writing a detailed journal of your estate planning journey.

5.   **Professional Assistance**: Don't hesitate to seek professional help. A financial advisor, attorney, or estate planner can offer tools and strategies for staying organized. It's like having a seasoned guide while trekking an uncharted trail.

6.   **Educate Your Successors**: Share your organizational strategies with your successor trustee or executor. They should be aware of how you've organized everything. It's like passing on the baton in a relay race; they need to know how to carry it forward.

7.   **Backup Plans: Always have a backup**. If you're using digital tools, ensure you have backups for your electronic data. In the physical realm, have copies of critical documents in a safe but accessible place.

8.   **Clear Labeling and Instructions**: Label all documents clearly and provide instructions if necessary. This will help your successors and family members understand your system and find what they need without confusion.

Remember, organization in estate planning isn't just about tidiness; it's about creating a seamless transition and ensuring that your wishes are carried out without unnecessary hurdles or delays. It's a gift of clarity and ease you give to yourself and those who will handle your affairs in the future.

7.4 Communication and Documentation

Navigating the complexities of estate planning requires two indispensable tools: meticulous documentation and clear communication. They're like the two oars of a boat, each equally important to keep you moving smoothly forward.

For both the testator and the successor trustee or executor, documentation is your compass. It guides every step of the journey, ensuring your decisions and actions align with the intended path. This is where your Letters of Instruction, as detailed in Section 2.10, become invaluable. They're not just directives; they are narratives that give context to your choices, explaining the 'why' behind the 'what.' It's like leaving behind a detailed map for those following in your footsteps.

However, a map is only as good as the traveler's ability to read it. This is where communication steps in. It's crucial to engage in various forms of communication – be it written, verbal, or digital. Regular updates, meetings, and correspondences help keep everyone on the same page. It's akin to a captain regularly updating their crew, ensuring everyone understands the course ahead.

But remember, communication isn't a one-off event. It's an ongoing process. Just like a ship's captain who must continually adjust their course based on new information, a trustee or executor must be ready to communicate changes, updates, and new developments. This consistent dialogue ensures that all parties involved – beneficiaries, legal advisors, and other stakeholders – are aligned and informed.

In essence, documentation and communication are the twin pillars that uphold the structure of effective estate planning. They work in tandem, with documentation providing the solid proof and historical record of decisions and actions, while communication ensures these actions are understood and accepted by all. Mastering both is crucial to steering the estate planning ship through calm and stormy waters alike. Remember, in the realm of estate planning, it's not just about making the right moves; it's also about clearly documenting and communicating those moves every step of the way.

7.5 Taxes

Welcome to the tax section of our journey! Ah, taxes – the part of life that's often as misunderstood as a teenager's moods, as feared as a dentist's drill, and, let's be honest, about as exciting as watching paint dry. But fear not! This section is designed to be your trusty guide through the murky waters of estate and tax planning. I have deliberately sprinkled some information here and there, a bit like repeating your favorite catchphrase, to ensure you grasp these essential concepts. Whether you're diving deep into the details or just skimming for the highlights, this part of the book is your roadmap to understanding taxes without the yawns. So, buckle up and let's make taxes a little less taxing!

Navigating the tax landscape as an executor is a crucial yet intricate aspect of your role. If the estate is substantial or the situation is complex, don't hesitate to bring on board a proficient probate lawyer and a certified public accountant, if necessary. It's important to remember that, as the executor, you're the one ultimately responsible for timely tax filing and payments. This includes both income and federal estate taxes, which are prioritized over most other debts. If you distribute assets before resolving tax obligations, you could find yourself personally on the hook for any unpaid taxes. Understanding the various taxes that might apply, considering the estate's value, income, and state laws, is essential. Always cross-check work done by professionals to ensure nothing slips through the cracks.

Here, I've outlined some key tax topics and included some commonly asked questions at the start. It's easy to feel overwhelmed by tax matters, especially if you're not a tax expert. The key is to know enough to ask your advisors the right questions and ensure you're getting accurate answers.

(a) Federal Income Tax
(b) Federal Estate Tax Exemptions
(c) The Gift Tax
(d) Generation-Skipping Transfer Tax
(e) Valuation of the Gross Estate
(f) Deductions
(g) Paying the Federal Estate Tax
(h) State and Local Income Tax
(i) State Death Taxes
(j) State Inheritance Taxes
(k) State Estate Taxes

ESTATE TAX FREQUENTLY ASKED QUESTIONS – FAQ QUICK GUIDE

What Is the Difference Between an Estate Tax and an Inheritance Tax?
In simple terms, think of the estate tax like a checkout fee on the total value of a grocery cart (the estate) right after someone's passing. It's like the government's share of the overall goods. The inheritance tax, on the other hand, is more like a personal tab each family member (beneficiary) has to pay on the specific items they receive from that cart. So, the estate itself covers the estate tax, while the inheritance tax is the individual bill each beneficiary settles.

What Is the Future of the Estate Tax?
The Tax Cuts and Jobs Act, like a game-changing rule in sports, significantly boosted the estate tax exemption to $11.18 million in 2018, with inflation adjustments each year. But, like a temporary bonus round in a game, this increase isn't permanent. Come January 1, 2026, we're back to the old rule – the exemption drops to its 2017 level of $5 million, again adjusting for

inflation. So, think of it like a window of opportunity with an expiration date, reminding us to plan wisely while the conditions are favorable.

How Much Can You Inherit from Your Parents Without Paying Taxes?
The location of an estate significantly influences its tax liability. Federally, estates worth less than $13.61 million in 2024 fall below the IRS threshold and are exempt from estate taxes. However, each state has its own rules regarding estate taxes, with varying thresholds and tax rates. Additionally, state-specific inheritance taxes may apply, affecting the amount received by beneficiaries. It's like a game where the rules change based on the location of the playing field, making it essential to understand both federal and state tax landscapes.

7.5 (a) Federal Income Tax

Handling the final tax innings for someone who's passed away is quite the responsibility. It's like being the closing pitcher in a baseball game, where the last inning can be as crucial as the first. The final tax return, covering income until the date of departure, is due on the regular Tax Day (usually around mid-April). It's like rounding the bases - you've got to touch them all, including any overdue returns.

If there's a surviving spouse, they can step up to the plate and file jointly, unless they've tied the knot again within the year. It's like changing teams mid-season; the rules shift to 'married filing separately.'

As for deductions, think of them like strategy plays in your tax game. Medical expenses exceeding a certain percentage of income (around 7.5%) can be deducted, but here's the twist - you can choose whether to deduct them from the income tax or the estate tax. However, just like a strategic play in sports, this move can't be used in both games. And remember, interest on savings bonds is a play you can call later, at redemption, unless you choose to report it as it builds up.

In the end, just like a good coach, it's about making the best calls for the team, considering all the plays available to you.

7.5 (b) Federal Estate Tax Exemptions

The federal estate tax exemption for 2024 is set at $13.61 million, up from $12.92 million in 2023, meaning only estate values above these thresholds are taxed. This exemption adjusts annually for inflation. It was significantly increased under the Tax Cuts and Jobs Act (TCJA) but is scheduled to expire post-2025 without further legislative changes. Married couples can combine exemptions, totaling $27.22 million. Estate tax rates can reach up to 40% for taxable amounts over $1 million, but they're applied progressively, so the rate depends on the specific amount exceeding the exemption.

7.5 (c) The Gift Tax

The gift tax is like a pre-game strategy where you pass on assets to your loved ones while you're still around. Think of it as a way to 'gift' a part of your legacy in advance. In 2024, you could give up to $18,000 per person per year without it counting against you. Here's the kicker: the gift tax and estate tax are on the same team, sharing the same exclusion limit. So, if you go overboard with your generosity during your lifetime, it might eat into the amount you can pass on tax-free when you're no longer here. It's all about playing the long game and balancing your giving now with what you'll leave behind later.

7.5 (d) Generation-Skipping Transfer Tax

The generation-skipping transfer (GST) tax is like a long pass in football, aiming to skip a generation. In 2023, the GST tax exemption was $12.92 million, hiking up to $13.61 million in 2024. Here's the deal: if you give more than this exemption amount to someone two generations down (like a grandchild), there's a flat 40% tax on the amount over the limit. It's important to note that these big generational passes also count towards your estate taxes, so they could attract both GST and estate taxes. It's like trying to dodge two defenders at once – tricky, but manageable with the right strategy.

7.5 (e) Valuation of the Gross Estate

Valuing an estate's gross assets is like setting a fair price in a market where both buyer and seller are well-informed and willing, without any pressure to transact. For securities, this is straightforward since their market value is regularly published. Real estate valuation involves comparing prices and tax assessments of similar properties, or getting an appraisal. For a solely owned business or professional practice, it's trickier. Here, the value hinges on a fair appraisal of all business assets, the business's proven earning potential, and other factors akin to evaluating corporate stock. When calculating taxes, you have the choice to value assets either at the date of death or six months later. This choice, made to potentially reduce tax obligations, is final once decided.

7.5 (f) Deductions

The unlimited marital deduction is like a financial lifeline, often sparing an estate from estate taxes by allowing all property passed to a surviving spouse – whether through wills, trusts, joint ownership, or insurance – to be exempt from estate tax. However, this can lead to tax challenges for the surviving spouse later on, as the inherited assets won't benefit from this deduction upon their passing, unless they remarry. Other deductions from the gross estate include funeral costs, estate administration expenses, paid estate debts, unpaid mortgages, losses during estate settlement, and charitable donations. These deductions can significantly reduce the taxable value of the estate.

7.5 (g) Paying the Federal Estate Tax

Paying the federal estate tax on time is crucial. Due within nine months after death, this payment is mandatory even if you get an extension to file the return. You might get a 12-month extension for the payment in challenging situations, or up to 10 years in specific cases, like when a closely held business forms a substantial part of the estate. Failing to make timely payments can lead to hefty penalties and interest. The IRS can also collect unpaid taxes from beneficiaries who've already received their shares, emphasizing the importance of timely and accurate estate tax management.

7.5 (h) State and Local Income Tax

Just like a team plays on different fields, you might have to tackle state and local taxes based on where the deceased lived. Think of it like adjusting your game plan for a home or away match. Each state or city can have its own set of rules for income tax, so it's like learning the local ground rules. It's crucial to check the playbook — in this case, the state and local tax laws — to understand your responsibilities, the taxes due, and the steps for filing those returns. Remember, each jurisdiction has its own unique tax terrain to navigate!

7.5 (i) State Death Taxes

In some states, there's either an inheritance tax (paid by beneficiaries) or an estate tax (paid by the estate itself). The inheritance tax is on the privilege of receiving property, and the closer the beneficiary's relation to the deceased, usually, the lower the tax rate and more exemptions available. The estate tax is levied for the privilege of transferring property at death. Both taxes apply to residents of the state, based on domicile - the permanent residence where the deceased most often lived, worked, and was registered to vote.

7.5 (j) State Inheritance Taxes

Some states implement an inheritance tax on either all or part of a deceased person's estate, which includes real estate within the state, irrespective of the deceased's actual residence, as well as all personal property owned by state residents. This inheritance tax is distinct in that it is levied on the beneficiaries rather than on the estate itself.

Beneficiaries are categorized into various classes for tax purposes. These classes typically include "Class A: Husband or Wife," "Class B: Immediate Family," and "Class C: All Others." Each of these classes faces different tax rates and exemptions. Generally, "Class A" beneficiaries, such as surviving spouses and immediate family members, benefit from the most generous exemptions and the lowest tax rates.

This classification system aims to tax inheritances more favorably for those beneficiaries who were closest to the deceased, recognizing the different levels of relationship between the deceased and the beneficiaries.

7.5 (k) State Estate Taxes

Even if the deceased's state doesn't levy an inheritance tax, the estate may still face a state estate tax. As of the date of publication, several states have a state estate tax in place, and more are contemplating adopting such a tax. This means as an executor, you might be required to file a state estate tax return. This requirement holds even in situations where no estate tax is payable.

The state estate tax is based on the privilege of transferring property upon death and differs from an inheritance tax, which is imposed on beneficiaries receiving property. Being aware of these nuances and complying with state-specific tax regulations is a crucial part of an executor's responsibilities.

7.6 Distribution and Final Accounting

Distribution: When it comes to distributing trust assets to the beneficiaries, the task kicks in after all the trust assets have been gathered, valued, and all debts and taxes settled. This is where the rubber meets the road in trust administration. The procedure mirrors that of distributing probate assets.

Before handing over any assets, make sure you get a signed receipt from each beneficiary. This is your proof of delivery, a crucial piece of evidence should any disputes arise later with other beneficiaries or creditors. Sometimes, the trust document will direct you to turn assets into cash before distribution, particularly if the majority are non-liquid like real estate or stocks. Your job here is to secure the best possible deal for these assets, liquidating them judiciously without gambling on market fluctuations.

However, there might be scenarios where selling off an asset isn't feasible or beneficial. For instance, if the trust includes a solely owned business or partnership share that's tough to sell in the open market, the practical solution could be to distribute the asset itself to the beneficiaries. In such cases, open and honest discussions with all beneficiaries are key to finding a solution that works for everyone. It's a balancing act, requiring tact and a firm grasp of both the trust document's instructions and the beneficiaries' expectations.

Final Accounting: As a successor trustee or executor, your role doesn't just conclude with the distribution of assets; it's also about maintaining clear and comprehensive documentation throughout the process. Before you consider your duties complete, it's prudent – and often legally necessary – to provide a final accounting to all trust beneficiaries or heirs. This final accounting is akin to a detailed summary of your management, documenting all income received and expenses incurred up to the point of settling the estate.

Securing a signed acknowledgment of this accounting from each beneficiary or heir is a critical step. Think of it as gathering confirmations, ensuring that everyone involved has reviewed, understood, and concurred with the financial narrative you've laid out. This acknowledgment acts as a protective measure, offering proof against any future claims of mismanagement or lack of transparency. It's essentially the closing chapter of your responsibilities, offering transparency and closure for all parties involved in the trust or estate.

Task	Details
Notify Stakeholders	Inform all beneficiaries and relevant parties of the start of closure proceedings.
Finalize Taxes	Ensure final personal, estate, and any other tax returns are filed and taxes paid.
Complete Asset Distribution	Distribute remaining assets as per the estate plan after all debts and taxes are paid.
Close Accounts	Terminate the estate's bank accounts and cancel any outstanding subscriptions or services.
Discharge Obligations	Pay any final expenses or debts associated with the estate.
Document Review	Ensure all estate-related documents are properly filed or recorded, including deeds and titles.
Court Approval	Obtain court approval for the final accounting and distribution if required by law.
Release Liens	Ensure all liens or encumbrances on estate property are released.
Final Accounting	Provide a detailed final accounting to beneficiaries and/or the court.
Archive Records	Securely store or archive estate records for the required period according to state laws.
Obtain Receipts	Get signed receipts from beneficiaries for distributions made.
Professional Consultation	Consult with an attorney to confirm all legal requirements have been met.
Confirm Estate Plan Fulfillment	Verify all terms of the will and/or trust have been fully executed.
Notify Probate Court	Inform the court of estate completion and seek formal discharge as executor.

This checklist is a general outline and does not encompass all specific legal and financial steps required in estate closure. Executors should seek professional advice to ensure compliance with all applicable laws and regulations.

Chapter 8

Reflecting on a Personal Journey – Lessons and Missteps

In this chapter, I delve into a deeply personal and raw reflection on the intricacies of family dynamics and estate planning, sharing my family's journey in navigating my father's legacy. My father crafted his estate with care, intending it as both a financial foundation and a testament to his love for us. His vision was clear: to leave a legacy that enhanced our lives and honored his values.

However, as time passed and my father aged, we witnessed the inevitable yet subtle changes in him, a journey familiar to many families. In retrospect, perhaps we were overly optimistic, not fully grasping the gradual shifts in his faculties. Late-life changes to his estate plan, though not ill-intentioned, significantly diverged from his original intent, raising questions about his mental state at the time and the motivations behind these alterations. This deviation not only muddled his intended legacy but also brought unforeseen complications and disappointments.

In this chapter, I don't seek to assign blame. Rather, I aim to share an honest account of our missteps and the lessons learned, sometimes in difficult ways. It's a tale of how well-meaning plans can falter without clear, realistic, and consistent vision. I share this narrative to offer insights into the complex process of estate planning, hoping to help others avoid the pitfalls we encountered.

By sharing these insights and experiences, I hope to guide others in their estate planning journey, which involves striking a balance between honoring your loved one's wishes and adapting to life's inevitable changes. Let this chapter serve as a beacon, helping you preserve and honor your family's legacy, mindful of the challenges and obstacles that might arise.

- **Failure of "Correct" Communication**: My father's adage, "Practice does not make perfect...CORRECT practice makes perfect," rings true in our family's communication challenges. Despite our efforts to hold family meetings, we failed to ensure mutual understanding. We could have employed multiple languages, outside interpreters, or other methods to guarantee a unified comprehension. It was awkward and inconvenient to address this issue, so we opted to do our best and hope for the best, which was a mistake.

- **Late-Life Marriages and Estate Planning**: My father's late-life marriage (at 85 years old), influenced by tax, financial security and property considerations, underscores the complexities in late-life marriages for estate planning. Any significant changes to a long-standing plan can have far-reaching, unintended consequences. It's crucial to be extra careful and clear about intentions in these situations, especially when dealing with advanced age and health issues like dementia.

- **Healthcare Decisions and Dementia**: My father's struggle with dementia added layers of confusion to our decision-making. Dementia's onset is unpredictable and erratic, leading us down many unproductive paths. It was a cycle of obsession, confusion, and frustration. Denial is a common reaction, yet acceptance and cohesiveness within the family are crucial. Difficult decisions need unanimous family support, and any reluctance or denial must be addressed head-on. We should have been more honest with ourselves and my father. We could have taken steps to protect him more when he needed it.

- **Family Dynamics and Estate Conflicts**: Different cultures have varied expectations about post-death practices. Misunderstandings about who should lead can arise, especially if the decedent's wishes contradict cultural norms. It's important to understand and discuss these cultural differences clearly.

- **Health Care & End of Life Decisions**: Opinions on end-of-life care vary widely. The most important aspect is to respect the wishes of the person nearing life's end. My father's choice of hospice care led to disagreements and misunderstandings within the family. Our inability to strongly advocate for his wishes resulted in unnecessary stress and conflicts, leaving a lasting impact even after his passing. More direct conversations and better documentation could have made this process smoother.

- **Forcing Business Partnerships Within the Family**: Blending business with family can be as complex as managing a team where everyone has a different playbook. My family's foray into a business relationship involved not just my siblings but their spouses as well. Even with clear roles, misunderstandings and hurt feelings emerged. In contrast, a client of mine chose to divide a substantial property into three parts, allowing each child to manage their own, thus avoiding the potential conflicts of joint management. This approach mirrors a coach tailoring training to each player's abilities. Another solution is appointing a third party to manage business affairs, much like a coach overseeing a team while players focus on their roles. These strategies underscore the importance of adapting estate planning to suit individual family dynamics and capabilities.

- **Planning Fatigue**: Reflecting on our latest round of estate planning, I'm reminded of the adage, "more haste, less speed." Our eagerness to cross the finish line overshadowed our focus on the journey itself. The process, admittedly exhausting and costly, bred a fervent desire in us to simply get it done, to put it behind us like a burdensome task. Yet, in our rush, we lost sight of a crucial aspect: the importance of meticulous attention to changes and details. The fatigue of planning, much like running a marathon, can blur the vision of even the most diligent. It's in these weary moments that critical details, those small yet significant cogs in the machinery of estate planning, can be overlooked. Our experience taught us a valuable lesson – the merit of taking a deep, calming breath amidst the storm of planning. Like an artist stepping back to view their painting, we needed to pause, to ensure each brushstroke of our estate plan accurately reflected our intentions.

Reflecting on our family's journey through estate planning, it's evident that even small missteps can significantly influence a legacy. Each error, whether an oversight or a miscommunication, contributed to a deviation from my father's intended legacy. This collective impact underlines the complexity of estate planning, which extends beyond financial and legal decisions to encompass emotional, cultural, and interpersonal family dynamics.

But wait ... there's more. I have also included some more common mistakes that might have been missed elsewhere. In the journey of estate planning, there are several common mistakes that, though not always front and center, significantly merit inclusion due to their potential impact. These mistakes can often be subtle and easily overlooked, yet they possess the capacity to profoundly alter the intended course of an estate plan. Along with the mistakes noted in other chapters (a summary of which has been provided below), each misstep can create ripples affecting the entire estate plan. It seemed logical to include these aspects here, to provide a more comprehensive understanding and to help others navigate these often-uncharted waters with greater awareness and caution.

Stupid, Easy Mistakes

We sometimes overlook the simplest tasks that can have profound impacts. Such oversights can derail even the most well-crafted plans, leading to outcomes that starkly contrast with the original intentions.

- **Losing Original Documents**: The mistake lies in misplacing or losing your will and original estate planning documents. Remember, digital copies are useful, but originals with "wet" signatures are crucial. To avoid this, securely store original documents and keep digital copies as backups in a safe, accessible location.

- **Not Reclaiming Documents from a Replaced Executor/Trustee**: Failing to retrieve original documents from a replaced executor or trustee is a common oversight. It's essential, albeit sometimes tricky, to ensure all crucial documents are returned. Proactively managing this transition can prevent complications.

- **Handwritten Wills and DIY Approaches**: The allure of handwritten or DIY wills is their simplicity, but they are fraught with risks, including errors in writing and execution. These can lead to significant legal issues. It's advisable to engage a professional to ensure the will is legally sound and accurately reflects your wishes.

- **Using a Codicil Instead of a New Will**: Opting for a codicil instead of drafting a new will can lead to confusion and potential legal challenges. If significant changes are needed, a new will is often clearer and more comprehensive.

- **Making Handwritten Changes Post-Execution**: Altering a will or trust with handwritten changes after it's been signed and witnessed is a mistake. These modifications may not be legally recognized. Amendments should be formally executed to maintain legal validity.

- **Impulsive Changes with a 'Quick and Dirty' Codicil**: Rushed changes through a hastily prepared codicil can create more problems than they solve. Thoughtful, well-drafted revisions are crucial to prevent disputes and ensure clarity.

- **Removing Staples from an Original Will**: This might seem trivial, but removing staples from an original will can raise questions about the integrity of the document. It's vital to keep the original document intact to avoid suspicions of tampering.

- **Neglecting Pet Care Provisions**: Overlooking arrangements for the care of your pets after death can leave them vulnerable. Including specific provisions for their care in your estate plan ensures they're looked after.

- **Duplicate Gifting of Tangible Property**: Assigning the same tangible property to multiple beneficiaries, either through vague descriptions or double allocation, is a mistake that can lead to disputes. Clear, specific descriptions and allocations are essential to avoid confusion.

- **Inadequate Provisions for Art and Collectibles**: Not properly planning for the disposition of artworks, collector's items, vintage cars, etc., can lead to valuation disputes and mishandling. Detailed instructions and appraisals can ensure these items are appropriately managed and distributed.

Real Estate Matters

Our journey underscored the importance of clear planning in real estate holdings. Decisions about maintaining, selling, or transferring properties can be laden with emotional and financial implications. Missteps in handling these assets can lead to significant tax burdens, legal complications, and familial discord.

- **Selling Property Close to Death**: Selling property shortly before death can result in missing out on tax advantages that death might provide, including step-up in basis and other legal benefits. To avoid this, consider the timing of property sales and consult with a tax professional about the potential implications of selling property close to the end of life.

- **Not Confirming Title Holding**: Failing to confirm how the title is held, either before or after death, can lead to unintended consequences in property distribution. Ensure clarity on title holding and make necessary adjustments to align with estate planning goals.

- **Overlooking Loans in Real Estate**: Forgetting that loans pass along with real estate is a common error. This can be problematic when the property value is less than the outstanding loan. Beneficiaries should be aware of the financial implications of inheriting such property.

- **Not Allowing Residence Continuation**: Failing to provide that children or others may continue to reside in the family home, subject to the executor or trustees' approval, can lead to unnecessary displacement and family strife. Including specific provisions in your estate plan can provide stability and continuity for loved ones.

- **Ignoring Lease Termination Provisions**: Not including provisions for the reasonable termination of leases after the property owner's death can create legal and financial complications. It's important to specify how leases should be handled to ensure smooth transitions and avoid disputes.

- **Owning Property in Foreign Countries**: Owning property in a foreign country can be complex, especially if the beneficiary is not a resident or lacks legal standing in that country. This can lead to legal and administrative challenges. Thorough planning and seeking legal advice in the respective country are crucial to navigate these complexities.

"More" Family Mistakes
Family dynamics are complex and can dramatically influence estate planning. In our experience, failing to communicate openly about the estate plan led to misunderstandings and unrealistic expectations. It's crucial to have honest conversations and manage expectations to maintain harmony and respect the true wishes of the benefactor.

- **Assuming Equal Rights for Step-Children**: A common mistake is assuming that step-children have the same legal rights as biological children in estate matters. To avoid ambiguity, be specific about the rights and inheritance of step-children in your estate planning documents.

- **Overlooking Spouse's Legal Rights**: Failing to consider a spouse's legal or statutory rights, such as the "Right of Election," can lead to unintended consequences. This right allows a surviving spouse to claim a portion of the estate, regardless of the will's contents. Ensure that your estate plan accounts for these rights to avoid legal complications.

- **Misconceptions About Divorce and Wills**: Assuming that a divorce automatically revokes your entire will is a mistake. In many jurisdictions, divorce may affect provisions concerning your ex-spouse but doesn't necessarily invalidate the entire will. It's crucial to review and update your will following a divorce.

- **Not Updating Will at Start of Divorce Proceedings**: Neglecting to update your will at the start of divorce proceedings can be risky. If you pass away during the process, your existing will remains effective, potentially leading to undesired outcomes. Update your will early in the divorce process to reflect your current wishes.

- **Ignoring Prenuptial Agreements in Wills**: Not mentioning or respecting the validity of prenuptial agreements in your will can create legal disputes. Ensure that your will aligns with the terms of any prenuptial agreements to uphold their validity and avoid challenges.

- **Disinheriting Out of Anger**: Disinheriting children or grandchildren due to anger or vindictiveness can lead to family strife and legal challenges. Consider the long-term impact of such decisions and explore alternatives like trusts or conditional bequests.

- **Failing to Name Disinherited Heirs**: Not specifically mentioning the names of heirs you intend to disinherit can lead to ambiguity and potential legal challenges. Explicitly stating your intentions in your will can help clarify your wishes and reduce disputes.

- **Excluding Long-Time Employees**: Overlooking long-time employees, such as secretaries or assistants, in your will, especially if they have been loyal and dedicated, can be an oversight. Consider including provisions for such individuals to acknowledge their contributions and support.

A Few "More" Tax Mistakes

Tax implications are often an afterthought, but they should be a forefront consideration. Our lack of foresight in tax planning resulted in avoidable financial burdens. Effective estate planning requires understanding and navigating the tax landscape to preserve the estate's value for beneficiaries.

- **Not Titling Assets in Both Spouses' Names**: A significant oversight in estate planning is not having assets titled in the name of each spouse. This can impact the utilization of each spouse's estate tax exemption amount. To maximize tax efficiency, it's essential to consider how assets are titled and whether they should be held jointly or separately. Proper titling can ensure that each spouse's estate tax exemption is fully utilized, potentially reducing the overall tax burden on the estate.

- **Overlooking Gift Tax Filings**: Failing to ascertain whether gift taxes were filed for substantial gifts can lead to tax compliance issues. When large gifts are made, it's crucial to file the appropriate gift tax returns, even if no tax is owed due to the lifetime exemption. Neglecting this step can result in penalties and complicate estate tax calculations. Regularly reviewing financial records and consulting with a tax professional can help ensure that all necessary tax filings are complete and accurate, maintaining compliance and avoiding unexpected liabilities.

In summary, estate planning is a careful balance that needs both technical expertise and a profound understanding of family dynamics. It involves crafting a legacy that resonates with an individual's values and wishes, while also considering the family's needs. Each decision, no matter its size, is a crucial component in the family's legacy tapestry. It's essential to approach these decisions with caution, clarity, and an awareness of their potential long-term impacts.

In light of these insights, it's worth reflecting on the 40 common mistakes outlined in this book. From failing to communicate effectively to overlooking family harmony, each mistake serves as a reminder of the nuances involved in estate planning. If you fear you might be making any of these errors, I encourage you to revisit the relevant sections for guidance. Remember, each step in estate planning, even a misstep, is an opportunity for growth and improvement in weaving the legacy you aspire to leave behind.

Mistake	Insight	Section
Treating estate planning as the whole game	Estate planning is one part of a broader financial strategy.	1.2
Failing to plan	Not planning can lead to undesired outcomes and complications.	1.3
Failing to avoid probate	Probate can be time-consuming and costly.	1.3
Starting with an attorney	Begin with clear goals before seeking legal advice.	2.1
Starting too late	Early planning is key to effective estate management.	2.1
Zeroing in solely on accumulating assets	Focus on wealth management, not just accumulation.	2.2
Choosing advisors based on personal relationships alone	Seek advisors with professional expertise, not just personal connections.	2.3
Not questioning the source of information or advice	Verify the credibility of your information sources.	2.3
Overemphasis on tax avoidance	Consider a balanced approach to estate planning, not just tax minimization.	2.4
Forcing philanthropy	Philanthropic decisions should align with personal values.	2.5
Failing to keep documents current	Regular updates are necessary to reflect life changes.	2.6

Neglecting document management and storage	Proper document management ensures accessibility and security.	2.6
Using the wrong tool	Choose estate planning tools that align with your goals.	2.7
Failing to spot a trigger event	Be alert to changes that might impact your estate plan.	2.8
Not keeping pace with technology	Embrace technological advances in estate planning.	2.1
Neglecting digital assets	Digital assets are an important part of modern estate planning.	2.1
Failing to Properly Fund Your Trust	Unfunded trusts fail to fulfill their purpose.	2.14
Ignoring the unique needs of your family	Tailor estate plans to your family's specific needs.	3.1
Overlooking cultural differences	Cultural considerations can significantly impact estate planning.	3.2
Forgetting emotional aspects	Emotional factors play a crucial role in estate planning.	3.3
Ignoring conflict flashpoints	Anticipate and plan for potential family conflicts.	3.4
Saying something only once	Repeat and clarify important information.	3.5
Disregarding family harmony	Prioritize maintaining peace within the family.	3.6
Failing to anticipate will challenges	Prepare for possible disputes over wills to avoid costly litigation.	3.6
Sidestepping fiduciary duties	Fulfilling fiduciary responsibilities is crucial for trustees and executors.	4.1
Overstepping boundaries	Respect the limits of your role in estate execution.	4.1
Short-sighted investments	Consider long-term implications in investment decisions.	4.1 (d)
Over-concentration and ignoring market changes	Diversify investments and stay informed about market trends.	4.1 (e)
Neglecting timely and accurate communication	Regular and clear communication is key in managing an estate.	4.1 (f)

Overlooking debts and expenses	Ensure all debts and expenses are accounted for and paid.	4.1 (g)
Inadequate or unfair distribution	Equitable distribution is essential for fairness and legal compliance.	4.1 (h)
Skipping final accounting	Complete and accurate accounting is necessary for transparency.	4.1 (i)
Choosing an executor based on birth order	Select executors based on capability, not just seniority.	4.2
Assigning co-executors without clear roles	Define specific roles to prevent conflicts and inefficiencies.	4.2
Not taking a fee	Consider accepting a fee for executor services to acknowledge the effort involved.	4.4
Underestimating the importance of communication and documentation	Effective communication and documentation are vital in estate management.	4.5
Neglecting professional advice	Seek and heed professional advice to avoid common pitfalls.	4.5
Overlooking emotional support	Emotional support is crucial during estate planning and execution.	5.1
Miscommunication about healthcare wishes	Clearly communicate and document healthcare preferences.	5.2
Ignoring personal grief	Recognize and address grief to make sound decisions.	5.3
Neglecting available resources	Utilize available resources for support and guidance.	5.4
Rushing decisions during initial grieving	Take time to process grief before making significant decisions.	6.1
Overlooking individual differences	Recognize and respect individual differences in grieving and decision-making.	6.3
Neglecting emotional well-being	Prioritize emotional health during estate planning and execution.	6.4

Chapter 9

Tools and Templates for Effective Legacy Planning

Chapter 9 of this book delves into the realm of "Tools and Templates for Effective Legacy Planning," a treasure trove of resources for those embarking on or already deep in the process of estate and legacy planning. In the digital age, the internet is awash with various tools, some intricately detailed and others offering a broad overview. However, it's essential to choose the right tool for the task at hand, just as you wouldn't use a backhoe for planting a small sapling.

My personal approach leans towards simplicity. The KISS (Keep It Simple, Stupid) philosophy is a guiding principle in my work. As someone who finds a unique pleasure in navigating spreadsheets (I've even been known to draft letters in Excel!), I've created a suite of tools designed to simplify and streamline the estate planning process. These tools, born out of my love for Excel and a desire to assist others on their journey, are available to anyone interested.

For those who prefer tangible resources, hard copies of these tools can be easily downloaded from my website, www.dgrealtyadvisors.com. If you're looking for interactive, working models that can be customized to your specific needs, feel free to contact my office via email or phone. I'll be more than happy to share them with you.

However, it's important to note that a basic familiarity with Excel is necessary to effectively utilize these tools. They are robust and can be incredibly helpful, but like any sophisticated tool, they can also be misused or "broken" if not handled with the requisite understanding and skill.

So, whether you're a seasoned estate planner or just starting out, Chapter 9 is designed to equip you with practical, easy-to-use resources to aid you in crafting a thoughtful and well-structured legacy plan.

Each of these tools is designed to streamline and simplify the estate planning process, offering a structured approach to what can be a complex and overwhelming task. Here's an overview of how each tool can benefit you:

1.   Profile: This tool helps you organize essential details about yourself and each family member. It's a centralized place to keep track of personal information, preferences, and unique characteristics, facilitating personalized estate planning.

2.   Account List: A comprehensive record of all your accounts and assets. This list ensures nothing is overlooked and assists in the smooth transfer of assets upon death.

3. **Big Questions:** A thought-provoking guide to help you ponder crucial aspects of estate planning, from personal values to legacy aspirations. This tool encourages a deep reflection on what you truly want to achieve with your estate plan.

4. **Terms:** This is a comprehensive glossary of key estate planning terms and definitions, serving as an invaluable resource for anyone new to the field. It helps in understanding and navigating through the often-complex jargon and technical language of estate planning. While this book also includes a glossary where I've tried to simplify definitions and infuse them with sports analogies to make the information more engaging and relatable, the "Terms" tool provides the traditional, more formal definitions. This dual approach ensures that whether you're looking for a straightforward explanation or a more colorful, sports-themed interpretation, you have the resources at hand to deepen your understanding of essential estate planning concepts.

5. **Locked Places**: A tool for documenting the locations of secure places (like safes or deposit boxes) and important security information, ensuring that your executor and beneficiaries know where to find and how to access crucial assets and documents.

6. **Questions FROM Executor:** A list of key queries an executor might have, helping them to efficiently carry out their duties with a clearer understanding of their role and responsibilities.

7. **Questions FOR Your Executor:** Essential questions to ask when selecting an executor. This helps in choosing the right person for this vital role, ensuring they align with your estate planning objectives.

8. **Timeline:** Outlines important milestones and timelines in the estate planning process, offering a structured approach to manage tasks and deadlines effectively.

9. **Key Documents**: A checklist of vital documents needed for comprehensive estate planning, ensuring all necessary paperwork is in order and easily accessible.

10. **Key Contacts**: Keep track of important contacts (like attorneys, accountants, and advisors) involved in your estate planning process. This tool helps maintain a network of professional support and ensures that critical contacts are readily available for your executor and family members.

These tools collectively aim to provide clarity, organization, and guidance throughout the estate planning journey, making it more manageable and less daunting for you and your loved ones.

Type	Last Name	First Name	Company Name	Phone	Email	Notes/Comments
Accountant - Estate Planning						
Accountant - Tax Prep & Business						
Attorney - Estate Planning						
Broker - Financial						
Broker - Mortgage						
Broker - Real Estate						
Family Member						
Friend						
Insurance Agent						
IT Support						
Property Manager						
Trustee						
Vehicle Repair						
Vendor (other)						
Vendor (other)						

Figure 9a: *Screen shot of excel based tool to help track key contacts.*

Type	Name	Created	Amended	Version Number/Nam	Location of File	Notes/Comment
Birth Certificate						
Business (Articles & Bylaws, etc.)						
Certification of Trust						
Deed						
Drivers License						
Educational						
Employment Agreement						
Funding Instructions						
Insurance						
Marriage/Divorce						
Military Document						
Nuptial Agreement						
Passport						
Powers of Attorney for Assets						
Powers of Attorney for Healthcare						
Pre or Post Marital Agreement						
Prepaid Funeral Contract						
Property Management						
Professional						
Promissory Notes						
Religious Ceremonial						
Schedules of Assets Directive to Trustees						
Settlement of Estate						
Tax						
Trust						
Will						

Figure 9b*: Screen shot of excel based tool to help track key documents.*

Type	Name / Company	Address	Notes/Comments
ALARMS			
Boat			
Business			
House			
Vehicle			
Other Alarm			
LOCKED PLACES			
Access Card/Code			
Combination Lock			
Computer Password			
Hiding Place			
Mini/Public Storage			
Post Office Box			
Safe - Private			
Safe-Deposit Box			
Things Needing Keys			
Other Password			

Figure 9c: Screen shot of excel based tool to help alarms and locked places.

II. Children & Grandchildren Information	Child ONE	Child TWO
Full Name		
Other Name/Nickname		
DOB		
Notes (Trust Role and considerations)		
Relationship (Birthchild or Adopted)		
Of Which Spouse/Partner (Both, Spouse ONE or Spouse TWO)		
Marital Status (if married list full name)		
Home Address		
Email Address		
Employer		
Occupation		
Does child have any special needs? Briefly explain.		
Name and dates of child's children (your grandchildren)		
Grandchild ONE Name / DOB		
Grandchild TWO Name / DOB		

Figure 9d: Screen shot of excel based tool to help track personal information.

1.0	Short-Term Cash & Equivalent	Bank or Institution	Name(s) on Account	Account #	Notes / Action Items
1.1	Cash				
1.2	Certif of Deposit (CDs)				
1.3	Checking / Savings				
1.4	Commodities (Gold, Silver, etc.)				
1.5	Money market				
1.6	Private Safe				
1.7	Rewards Program				
1.8	Safe Deposit Box				
1.9	Treasury Bills (T-bills)				
1.10	Other Cash Equiv.				

2.0	Liabilities	Bank or Institution	Name(s) on Account	Account #	Notes / Action Items
2.1	Auto loans				
2.2	Basic Living Expense				
2.3	Business Loans				
2.4	Child Support				
2.5	Credit Card Debt				
2.6	Home equity loans/LOC				
2.7	Legal Judgments/ liens				
2.8	Mortgage				
2.9	Personal Debts				
2.10	Student loans				
2.11	Tax liabilities				
2.12	Rent				
2.13	Other Liabilities				

3.0	Retirement Savings	Bank/Institution	Name(s) on Account	Account #	Notes / Action Items
3.1	401(k) plans				
3.2	Education Savings				
3.3	Defined Benefit Plans				
3.4	Individual Retirement Accounts (IRAs)				
3.5	Pension				
3.6	Retirement annuities				
3.7	Social Security				
3.8	Other Retirement				

4.0	Securities	Bank/ Institution	Name(s) on Account	Account #	Notes / Action Items
4.1	Annuities				
4.2	Certif of Deposit (CDs)				
4.3	Commodities Securities				
4.4	Exchange-Traded Funds (ETFs)				
4.5	Foreign Currencies				
4.6	Mutual Funds				
4.7	Options				
4.8	Stocks & Bonds				
4.9	Treasury Securities				
4.10	Unit Invest Trusts (UITs)				

5.0	Personal Items	Item	Name(s) on Account	ID Number	Notes / Action Items
5.1	Artwork				
5.2	Auto				
5.3	Collections				
5.4	Furniture				
5.5	Jewelry				
5.6	Other Personal Items				
5.7					

6.0	Other Assets	Item	Name(s) on Account	Account #	Notes / Action Items
6.1	Crypto & Digital Assets				
6.2	Deferred Comp				
6.3	Foreign Assets				
6.4	Goodwill				
6.5	Inheritance (Received or Expected)				
6.6	Insurance - Auto				
6.7	Insurance - Disability				
6.8	Insurance - Property				
6.9	Insurance - Life				
6.10	Insurance - Medical				
6.11	Intellectual Prop. (TM, Patents, Copyrights)				
6.12	Money Owed to You				
6.13	Royalties				
6.14	Other Assets/Ins.				

7.0	Business Interests & W2 Inc.	Business Name	Name(s) of Owners	Manager/ Contact	Notes / Action Items
7.1	Corporation				
7.2	Franchise Ownership				
7.3	Joint Venture				
7.4	Nonprofit				
7.5	Partnership				
7.6	Sole Proprietorship				
7.7	Trust Fund				
7.8	W2 Employment				
7.9	Other Income				

8.0	Property	Property Address	Name(s) on Title	Manager/ Contact	Notes / Action Items
8.1	Family Home				
8.2	Timeshare				
8.3	Vacation Property				
8.4	Other Personal Property				

	Investment Property	Property Name / Address	Name(s) on Title	Market Value / Loan	Notes / Action Items
9.1	Comm. Prop (Office, Retail, Warehouses)				
9.2	Residential Property (SFR, Condos, Apart)				
9.3	Medical or Healthcare Facilities				
9.4	Self-Storage Facilities				
9.5	Senior or Assisted Living				
9.6	Student Housing				
9.7	Vacant Land				
9.8	Vacation or Short-term Rental				
9.9	Other Inv. Property				

10.0	Other Prop Investments	Property Name/ Address	Name(s) on Title	Manager/ Contact	Notes / Action Items
10.1	Delaware Statutory Trusts (DSTs)				
10.2	Real Estate Investment Trusts (REITs)				
10.3	Real Estate Limited Partnerships (RELPs)				
10.4	Real Estate Syndications				
10.5	Other RE Investments				

Figure 9e: Screen shot of excel based tool to help track financial information.

Chapter 10
Conclusion and Reflections

As we close this book, it's important to reflect on the journey we've taken together. Throughout these pages, we've navigated the complexities of estate and legacy planning, understanding it's not just about distributing assets, but about passing on a legacy that embodies our values, hopes, and aspirations.

You've been introduced to the intricacies of family dynamics, the importance of effective communication, and the necessity of choosing the right executor or successor trustee. We've delved into the nuances of taxes, documentation, and organization, all while recognizing the emotional weight these decisions carry.

In sharing my family's experiences, both the triumphs and the missteps, I've laid bare the reality that estate planning is a deeply personal and often challenging journey. It's a journey that requires not just financial acumen but emotional intelligence, a deep understanding of your family, and the foresight to anticipate and navigate potential conflicts.

But beyond the technicalities and the strategies, this journey is fundamentally about legacy – what we leave behind, not just in material wealth, but in memories, values, and the foundations we lay for future generations. It's about crafting a story that continues long after we're gone, one that speaks to who we were and what we stood for.

As you continue on your own journey, remember that estate planning is a continuous process, evolving as your life and circumstances change. It requires regular revisiting and updating, much like revising a life-long game plan.

Take heart in knowing that by engaging in this process, you've already begun the critical work of shaping your legacy. It's a testament to your foresight and care for those you'll one day leave behind.

I encourage you to approach this journey with both diligence and heart. Remember, estate planning is not just a task to be completed but an ongoing conversation about life, love, and legacy. It's a conversation that, though it may start with you, will continue through the lives and stories of those you love and leave behind.

Remember that estate and legacy planning is about more than assets and legal documents; it's about crafting a story of your life, values, and love – a story that will be told through the lives of those you hold dear. As you step forward, do so with the knowledge that your actions today will shape the memories and legacies of tomorrow.

Glossary

In estate planning, understanding various terms is like knowing the rules of a game. Here's a simplified glossary with a sports analogy twist (as mentioned in Chapter 9, Practical Tools, you can download more traditional terms on my website):

AB Trust: Like a relay race baton, it passes assets from one spouse to another, then to the kids, avoiding estate tax.

Accounting: A scorecard of an estate's assets, income, and expenses.

Acknowledgment: A notary's verification, like a referee confirming a goal.

Administration: Managing an estate, akin to a coach strategizing a team's play.

Administration Expenses: Costs of running the estate, like a team's operational expenses.

Administrator: The court-appointed 'captain' handling an estate.

Advancement: An advance on inheritance, like a pre-game bonus.

Affiant: Someone swearing an oath, like a player taking a sportsmanship pledge.

Affidavit: A written, sworn statement, like a signed player contract.

After-born Child: A child born after a will's creation, like a late draft pick.

Agent: A person acting on behalf of another, like a player's agent.

Alternate Beneficiary: A backup inheritor, like a reserve player.

Alternate Valuation Date: A later date to value estate assets, like a postponed game's new date.

Anatomical Gift: Donating organs, like donating gear to a sports club.

Ancillary Probate: Probate in a non-primary residence state, like an away game.

Annual Gift Tax Exclusion: Tax-free gift limit, like a salary cap.

Attestation Clause: Witnesses' confirmation of a will's signing, like a team's endorsement.

Attorney at Law: A legal representative, akin to a coach.

Attorney in Fact: An agent in legal matters, like a player's representative.

Basis for Tax Purposes: Value assessment for tax, like a player's market value.

Beneficiary: An inheritor, like a winning team's shareholder.

Bequeath: To leave personal property in a will, like passing a cherished jersey.

Bequest: A personal property gift in a will, like a trophy handover.

Bond: A financial guarantee, like a safety net for a team.

Bypass Trust: Skips the surviving spouse's estate, like passing the ball to the next player.

Charitable Remainder Trust: Benefits you, then a charity, like playing first then coaching.

Charitable Trust: Funds a charity, like sponsoring a sports event.

Codicil: A will's amendment, like a rule change in a game.

Co-executor: Joint estate manager, like co-captains.

Common Disaster: Simultaneous death scenario, like a team facing a shared challenge.

Community Property: Jointly owned marital property, like a team-owned stadium.

Conditional Gift: A gift with terms, like conditional player contracts.

Conservator: Manager for a minor's property, like a junior team's coach.

Contingent Beneficiary: An inheritor if the primary can't inherit, like a substitute player.

Convenience Account: An account for easy access, like a reserve fund for quick use.

Creditor: Someone owed money, like a team owing to a vendor.

Custodian: A minor's property manager, akin to a youth coach.

Death Tax: Tax on inheritance, like a transfer fee.

Debtor: Someone owing money, like a team in debt.

Decedent: The deceased, akin to a retired player.

Decree: A court's order, like a league's ruling.

Deed: A property title transfer document, like passing the ownership baton.

Descendant: An inheritor down the family line, like a legacy player.

Devise: Real property gift in a will, like bequeathing a sports club.

Disclaimer: Refusal of inheritance, like declining a player transfer.

Discretionary Trust: Trust with flexible distributions, like a coach's discretionary picks.

Disinherit: Excluding from inheritance, like cutting a player from the team.

Distribution: Handing out estate assets, akin to award distribution.

Domicile: Primary residence state, like a home ground.

Donee: Gift recipient, like a sponsored athlete.

Donor: Gift giver, akin to a team sponsor.

Dower and Curtesy: Surviving spouse's inheritance right, like a retired player's pension.

Durable Power of Attorney: Retains validity if the grantor is incapacitated, like a player's contract valid through injuries.

Escheat: Estate goes to the state if no heirs.

Estate: All the assets you own, like a player's career stats and trophies.

Estate Planning: Crafting a game plan for managing and passing on your assets.

Estate Tax: Like a transfer fee, it's the tax on transferring property at death.

Executor: The coach managing your estate, ensuring your game plan is followed.

Family Allowance: Immediate funds for family, akin to a team's emergency fund.

Fiduciary: Trusted team manager responsible for overseeing someone else's assets.

Forced Share: A surviving spouse's guaranteed portion of the estate, like a contractually obligated bonus.

Funding a Trust: Transferring assets to a trust, like signing over a player to a new team.

Generation-Skipping Tax: Tax on assets passed directly to grandchildren, bypassing a generation.

Generation-Skipping Trust: A strategy to benefit multiple generations while dodging repeated estate taxes.

Gift: Transferring property without expecting something in return, like a free jersey giveaway.

Gift Tax: Tax on substantial gifts given during life, similar to luxury taxes in sports.

Gift Tax Exclusion: The amount you can gift without incurring taxes, like a salary cap.

Grantor: Person setting up a trust, like a team founder.

Grantor Trust: A trust where the founder keeps some control and tax responsibility.

Gross Estate: Total value of your assets, without debts, like a player's gross worth.

Guardian ad litem: Court-appointed advocate for minors or incompetents, like a player's agent.

Guardian of Person/Property: Court-appointed caretaker for a person or their assets.

Heir: Someone legally entitled to inherit, like a rookie inheriting a star player's position.

Holographic Will: A handwritten will, like a player's handwritten contract. California is a state that will potentially recognize a handwritten will as being valid, provided they meet certain requirements.

Income Beneficiary: Someone who gets income from a trust, but not the trust assets.

Incompetent: Legally unable to handle affairs, like a player sidelined by injury.

Inherit: Receiving property from someone who passed away, like inheriting a jersey number.

Inheritance Tax: State tax on receiving an inheritance, like a signing bonus tax.

Insolvent Estate: When estate debts exceed assets, like a team in financial trouble.

Insurance Trust: A trust managing life insurance payouts.

In-terrorem Clause: A clause that disinherits anyone who challenges the will or trust.

Intervivos Trust: A trust created during the grantor's lifetime.

Intestacy Laws: Rules for asset distribution when there's no will.

Intestate: Dying without a valid will, like a game without a rulebook.

Inventory: Listing all estate assets, like a team's roster and equipment inventory.

Irrevocable Trust: A trust that can't be changed after creation.

Issue: Descendants, like a sports dynasty's future generations.

Joint Ownership: Owning property together, like co-owning a team.

Joint Tenant: Co-owner in joint ownership.

Joint Will: A single will for multiple people, not recommended due to potential issues.

Lapsed Gift: A failed gift in a will or trust because the recipient died first.

Letter of Instruction: An informal guide for survivors on personal and estate matters.

Letters of Administration/Testamentary: Legal authority to administer an estate.

Residuary Beneficiary/Estate: Person/property receiving anything left after specific gifts.

Revocable: Can be changed or cancelled.

Revocable Trust: A trust that can be altered or ended by the grantor.

Right of Survivorship: Joint owner automatically getting ownership upon co-owner's death.

Self-proving Will: A will with a sworn statement from witnesses, confirming its validity.

Separate Property: Spouse-owned property, not jointly owned.

Settlor: Person who establishes a trust.

Simultaneous Death Clause: Rules for property distribution if it's unclear who died first.

Small Estate: An estate small enough for simplified legal procedures.

Sole Ownership: Owning property alone, like a sole team owner.

Special Needs Trust: Supports a disabled beneficiary without affecting government aid.

Specific Bequest: A gift of specific property to a named beneficiary.

Spendthrift Clause/Provision: Protects trust assets from being misused or taken by creditors.

Spousal Share: The part of an estate a surviving spouse is legally entitled to.

Sprinkling Trust: Trust giving the trustee discretion on how to distribute income.

Standby Trust: Like a reserve player, it's an unfunded trust ready to step in when needed.

State Death Tax Credit: A tax offset, similar to a sports team getting a credit for playing home games.

Statute of Descent and Distribution: Rules dictating how an estate is divided, like the league's guidelines for distributing trophies.

Stepped-up Basis: Updated tax value at death, akin to a player's value reassessed after a standout season.

Succession: Inheriting property, like a rookie stepping up to a veteran's role.

Successor Trustee: The person who takes over trust management, like a new coach taking over a team.

Summary Probate: A simpler estate process for small estates, like a fast-tracked rookie contract negotiation.

Taking Against the Will: A spouse choosing a legal share over the will's offer, like a player opting for the standard contract instead of a special deal.

Tangible Personal Property: Physical items like artwork or furniture, similar to sports equipment.

Taxable Estate: The portion of an estate subject to tax, like taxable income for a player.

Tenancy by the Entirety: Joint ownership for married couples, like co-captains in a team.

Tenancy in Common: Joint ownership without survivorship rights, like teammates owning a business together.

Tenants by the Entirety/Tenants in Common: Co-owners in a property, akin to team members with shared or individual stakes.

Testamentary: Relating to a will, like rules specific to post-game scenarios.

Testamentary Trust: A trust created by a will, like a strategy devised for future games.

Testate: Having a valid will at death, like a player retiring with a solid game plan.

Testator: Person who makes a will, like a team captain devising a game strategy.

Totten Trust: A bank account that passes to a beneficiary, like a player's savings plan for retirement.

Transfer-on-Death (TOD) Designation: Naming a beneficiary to inherit assets, bypassing probate, like passing a jersey number to a chosen successor.

Trust: A legal arrangement managing property for another's benefit, akin to a team's trust fund.

Trustee: Manager of a trust, like a team's general manager.

Trustor: The creator of a trust, akin to a team founder.

Undue Influence: Pressuring someone to sign a legal document against their will, like a player coerced into signing an unfair contract.

Unfunded Trust: A trust without assets, like a team without players.

Unified Credit: A tax credit against estate and gift taxes, like a salary cap exception.

Uniform Anatomical Gift Act: Law for body and organ donation, like rules for sports gear donations.

Uniform Gifts to Minors Act: Law for gifting to minors, similar to junior sports scholarships.

Uniform Probate Code (UPC): Standardized probate laws, akin to uniform rules in sports leagues.

Uniform Prudent Investors Act: Guidelines for executors and trustees on investing, like a playbook for financial management.

Uniform Transfers to Minors Act: Rules for transferring property to minors, similar to passing a sports legacy to a younger player.

Will: A document outlining asset distribution after death, like a player's post-career plans.

Witness: Someone verifying a legal document's signing, akin to a referee confirming a score.

Wrongful Death Claim: A legal claim for someone's death, like a penalty for a game-related injury causing harm.

About The Author

Tim Gorman is a multifaceted professional who combines his expertise as a licensed Real Estate Broker, a former Certified Public Accountant (CPA, inactive), and a seasoned entrepreneur to provide insightful guidance in the realms of real estate and estate planning. His journey in the real estate world commenced in 2010 when he became a part of WR Gorman & Associates, a brokerage firm based in Brea, California, joining forces with his father to continue a legacy of wealth-building through real estate.

In a tribute to this legacy and with a commitment to offering customized real estate solutions, Tim co-founded DG Realty Group, Inc., alongside Nicholas Dunlap. Their venture focuses on full brokerage services, underscoring Tim's extensive experience and expertise as a broker and a successor trustee.

Tim's career trajectory is highlighted by significant roles and achievements, showcasing his diverse skill set. He has served as a senior auditor at KPMG, where his responsibilities included providing comprehensive guidance and detailed analysis for major national accounts. His executive experience extends to key roles in marketing, funds administration, and strategic planning within a publicly held corporation, in addition to being the director of national marketing for a company with an extensive network spanning 29 states and 11 countries. His entrepreneurial spirit is further demonstrated through his involvement as a founding partner in various ventures, including restaurants, consulting firms, and a youth sports league.

As an author, Tim has made notable contributions to the field of real estate and estate planning. He has authored "Your Legacy & Real Estate Assets: A Guide to Planning Your Legacy" and contributed to "Cash-In on the Myths of Real Estate" by William R. Gorman. Beyond his books, Tim is a frequent contributor to the Apartment News Magazine, a publication of the Apartment Association of Orange County, where he shares his insights and expertise with a wider audience. His work in these publications reflects his deep understanding of and experience in real estate, finance, and estate planning.

Tim is passionately committed to sharing the essential lessons gleaned from his experiences as a real estate broker, investor, successor trustee, and executor. He aims to empower individuals with the knowledge and strategies needed for effective estate planning and real estate investment.

For inquiries, advice, or comments, Tim Gorman can be contacted through his website at:

http://www.dgrealtyadvisors.com

or via email at:

info@dgrealtyadvisors.com

www.ingramcontent.com/pod-product-compliance
Lightning Source LLC
Chambersburg PA
CBHW082234220526
45479CB00005B/1223